COLLABORATIVE BRIDGES

PEOPLE, PLACES & THINGS

Aileen Kirkham

UpstartBooks™

Fort Atkinson, Wisconsin

*To the Texas Menoposse Writers' Group—Pat Miller and Jackie Hopkins—
and to the best high school English teacher anyone could ever have—
Mrs. Myers. Last, but not least, to beloved friend and teacher,
the late Mrs. Jimmie Doerge.*

*I hope this book will ignite and inspire the endless learning potential of
children and of those who educate them.*
—Aileen Kirkham

K–8 national standards determined by McREL (Mid-continent Research for Education and Learning, www.mcrel.org). Standards © McREL, 2004.

Published by UpstartBooks
W5527 State Road 106
P.O. Box 800
Fort Atkinson, Wisconsin 53538-0800
1-800-448-4887

© Aileen Kirkham, 2005
Cover design: Debra Neu

Dewey, DDC and Dewey Decimal Classification are registered trademarks of OCLC Online Computer Library Center, Incorporated.

The paper used in this publication meets the minimum requirements of American National Standard for Information Science — Permanence of Paper for Printed Library Material. ANSI/NISO Z39.48-1992.

All rights reserved. Printed in the United States of America.
The purchase of this book entitles the individual librarian or teacher to reproduce copies for use in the library or classroom. The reproduction of any part for an entire school system or for commercial use is strictly prohibited. No form of this work may be reproduced or transmitted or recorded without written permission from the publisher.

Contents

Introduction

Motivation

My motivation for writing this series is a result of some very relevant collaborations:

- Upstart's informal survey of what librarians desire to purchase to support the emphasis on instructional collaborations between librarians and teachers.

- My longtime friendship and prior collaborations with Pat Miller while doing professional in-services, children's programming and as fellow wordsmiths in our Texas Menoposse Writers' Group. (Pat is the author of the Stretchy Library Lessons series and is my co-author on the Collaborative Bridges series.)

- The inspiration of hearing an author saying she was enamored with the fact that her editor offered her the possibility of doing a trilogy—my editor has, too!

How to Use This Book

Collaborative Bridges: People, Places & Things provides dynamic lessons and activities with curriculum connections that can be taught in the library or the classroom or as the best of both instructional formats: a collaborative effort between the librarian and classroom teachers. With each unit having two complete lessons and the bridges activities that complement the lesson's topic, the Collaborative Bridges series offers the flexibility of mixing and matching lessons and activities to address a variety of elementary curriculum objectives and student learning styles. The units are composed of interactive instruction and facilitation via question and answer strategies, discussion, book studies, games, Internet research, kid-friendly activities, role-playing, time lines, diverse perspectives, graphic organizers, holiday crafts, DVDs, videos, CDs and hands-on projects.

Each Collaborative Bridges Lesson Includes:

McRel Standards. The McRel Standards were developed by Mid-Continent Research for Education and Learning in Aurora, Colorado. McRel was incorporated in 1966 to "help educators ... bridge the gap between research and practice." The full list of standards can be found at www.mcrel. org/standards-benchmarks. The activities in this book are primarily based on social studies objectives, but also incorporate the following language arts standards:

- Writing

  - Uses the general skills and strategies of the writing process.

  - Uses the stylistic and rhetorical aspects of writing.

  - Uses grammatical and mechanical conventions in written compositions.

- Gathers and uses information for research purposes.

- Reading
  - Uses the general skills and strategies of the reading process.
  - Uses reading skills and strategies to understand and interpret a variety of literary texts.
  - Uses reading skills and strategies to understand and interpret a variety of informational texts.

- Listening and Speaking
  - Uses listening and speaking strategies for different purposes.

- Viewing
  - Uses viewing skills and strategies to understand and interpret visual media.

- Media
  - Understands the characteristics and components of the media.

Objectives. The standards are broad national guidelines. Objectives are more measurable and more directly tied to curriculum. Space has been left for you to include local objectives.

Rationale. Reasons these particular lessons were selected to meet the standards and objectives.

Library Lesson. The library lesson can be completed in one or two 20-minute sessions.

Bridge Activities. These activities can be used to extend the library or classroom learning. They can be used as stand-alone lessons or as a bridge in the collaborative plans of the media specialist and teacher. They can be used in any order, or in place of the library or classroom activities.

Classroom Lesson. The classroom lesson is a longer lesson that is often a culmination of the lesson introduced in the library. It is completed by the classroom teacher, but can be expanded through planning with the librarian.

Resources. Materials were chosen to represent multicultural themes and to appeal to many learning styles. Fiction and nonfiction titles are listed for every unit, as well as multimedia and Internet resources. Due to restrictive library budgets, the media listed in the bibliography includes titles from established collections and many newer releases. Put these or similar books on display near your teaching area. Bookmark the sites on your library computer and/or send them home on a bookmark for students to use on home or public library computers. The Web sites are current as of this printing, but if you get an error message, perform a key word search on the Web site title.

Unit 1
Presidents: Past & Present

McRel Standards

Economics

* Understands the roles the government plays in the United States economy.

History

* Understands how democratic values came to be and how they have been exemplified by people, events and symbols.

Objectives

* Participate in a news interview.

* Use dictionaries and thesauri to generate an A-Z list of admirable presidential personality and leadership traits.

* Write an original quotable quote that a president could have said.

* Define the meaning of character assassination/slander and how it can be prevented in political campaigning.

* Create an original commercial for a political campaign.

* Research the positive and negative attributes of past presidents' terms in office and write a newspaper article with supporting details as to whether or not the president deserved to be in the Hall of Fame, on the Wall of Shame or both.

Local Objectives

_____

_____

_____

_____

Rationale

Students, as future voters in a global society, need to gain a basic understanding of the leadership characteristics a president should have, the election process and how past presidents have impacted America's history.

 **Library Lesson**
A Kid's Campaign

Prepare in Advance:

Read *The Kid Who Ran for President* and make the spotlight and interview cards. Use the Spotlight on the Candidate template on page 13 to make a transparency. Make news media interview cards using pages 14–18. The cards are easily visible if they are enlarged so that each card is one quarter of a sheet of poster board. If you like, dress in character as an elementary school boy and use a boy's voice to do the interview.

Lesson Directions:

Explain to the students that some of them will receive a card with a question on one side and the name of a media company on the other. Tell them that if they get a card, they should hold it up when the visiting book character says, "Questions, please." (The character only has to say this a few times for the students to understand the interview format.) Tell the students that as soon as the character starts to answer the question, they should hold the cards in their laps until it is time for the next question. After a student's question is answered, he or she should not hold the question up again. Demonstrate this procedure for students and link it to their prior knowledge by referencing news conferences they've seen on television. Pass out the interview cards for kids to practice reading. Perform the press conference. Present the interview. (Answers to the Interview Cards are provided on page 19.) **Optional:** Before the interview, set the atmosphere by playing "Hail to the Chief" from the *Patriotic Songs & Marches* CD.

Note: This presentation provides the opportunity for students to practice creating their own book presentations and gaining public speaking skills.

Discuss the pros and cons of a kid running for president from the students' class. (To clarify basic eligibility, read aloud page 13 from *The Presidents of the United States*.) If the teacher wishes to do this as a collaborative lesson, provide a class set of *The Kid Who Ran for President* for the class to read in preparation for the classroom lesson.

Bridge Activity 1
The ABCs of the Presidency

Share that the class will create an A-Z listing of George Washington's personality and leadership traits. Read *George Washington's Teeth* aloud, then record student responses from A-Z. If students need more background on Washington to generate the list, read aloud Washington's information in *Lives of the Presidents: Fame, Shame (and What the Neighbors Thought)*. Encourage the use of classroom dictionaries, thesauri and Web sites (yahooligans.yahoo.com/reference/thesaurus and wordcentral.com/ are helpful) to generate the list (e.g., Active, Brave, Courageous, Daring, etc.).

Pass out the ABC bookmark pattern from page 20. Explain that the students should create a bookmark with the same ABC format and adjectives to describe themselves as if they were the kid who ran for president. (They can continue on the back of the bookmark if necessary.) Have students read aloud their ABC's and post them on a classroom bulletin board.

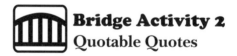

Bridge Activity 2
Quotable Quotes

Define and give examples of quotable quotes from Suzy Red's Web site: www.suzyred.com/quotes.html.

Share a quote(s) from *Lincoln: A Photobiography*, pages 133–137. Direct students to watch the *Abraham Lincoln* video, and listen for any quotable quotes. After watching the video, brainstorm with students the words to finish the following phrase:

If Abraham Lincoln came back today, this is the quote he would want to say: _____.

Record student responses. Challenge students to write one quotable quote they would use if they were the kid who ran for president. Have students read aloud their quotes, then post them on a bulletin board or in a class book of quotable quotes.

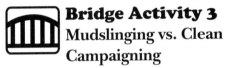 **Bridge Activity 3**
Mudslinging vs. Clean Campaigning

Display the phrase "character assassination" and ask the students to guess what it means. To correct or confirm this answer, visit hyperdictionary.com/dictionary/character+assassination. Read the definition aloud and discuss what it means. (Most students will think it means someone is dead.) Discuss the mudslinging in Judson Moon's (the main character in *The Kid Who Ran for President*) campaign. Tell the students that as you read an excerpt from the book, they need to listen for the group of people that Judson slandered. (Students may not know the word "slander." Explain that it is a synonym for "mudslinging." It is important that kids search for meaning and definition by reading in context.) Read the excerpt from page 69, beginning with the paragraph "I'm sure you're aware of the problems our country faces today ..." Stop the reading with the paragraph on page 71 that ends "... President in 2000. And Win!" Brainstorm where Judson could have gotten accurate information to become informed on the issues and what kind of statements he should have used to give a clean campaign speech.

 **Bridge Activity 4**
It Pays to Advertise

Display a variety of promotional buttons, pins, posters, newspaper ads and magazine articles and ask students why it pays to advertise. Record all reasons. Ask the students why it is necessary for presidents and presidential candidates to advertise constantly. Share some pages from *The Buck Stops Here* and note that the pages look like pages of magazine ads for campaign advertising. Tell the students that you have decided to run for president. Because you need a quality advertising campaign for your candidacy, the students will be divided into three or four groups—or advertising agencies—trying to get your campaign business. Their objective is to create a commercial to help you win. Give them specific criteria for creating the commercial.

Suggested criteria:

- 1 minute long
- may use props and/or music
- must be a clean campaign ad with no mudslinging
- all group members must participate

Videotape the commercial presentations, play them back for students and provide your professional critique and rationale as to which one you will pick for your campaign.

 Classroom Lesson
Presidents in Residence—Hall of Fame vs. Wall of Shame

Make transparencies of pages 21 and 22. Direct the students to discern whether presidents should make the list for the Hall of Fame, the Wall of Shame or both by listening to two excerpts from *Lives of the Presidents: Fame, Shame (and What the Neighbors Thought)*: pages 11–13 (George Washington) and page 53 (Warren G. Harding—you may want to skip last sentence depending on the maturity of your students). Have the students vote on which category(s) a president should be placed in, then mark an "X" in the column(s).

Point out that there was very little media influence in the earliest elections. Discuss how news media can strongly impact voters. Have the kids think of a name for a classroom newspaper and vote on the name. Then assign each student a president and have him or her write an article for the classroom newspaper. As editor of the newspaper staff you must specify your editorial criteria for the articles: vital statistics of birth, years in office, marital status, number of children and at least three facts with supporting details as to why the president's term in office was successful, not successful or some of both. The students must use at least three different sources of information and provide a modified bibliography to verify research. Publish the reports in the class newspaper. Allow students time to read the newspaper, then have the class vote on the category(s) to mark on the transparency.

 **Resources**
Books

Fiction

The Kid Who Became President by Dan Gutman. Scholastic, 1999. 4–5. Sequel to *The Kid Who Ran for President*.

The Kid Who Ran for President by Dan Gutman. Scholastic, 1996. 4–5. With the help of his politically savvy classmate, a 12-year-old class clown runs for president.

Marvin Redpost: Class President by Louis Sachar. Random House, 1999. 3–4. A visit from the president results in humor, good citizenship and celebrity status for a third grade class.

Nonfiction

The Buck Stops Here: The Presidents of the United States by Alice Provensen. HarperCollins, 1990. 3–6. Mixed format book with banner style pages featuring presidents through Clinton and events of their presidencies with mini-biographical pages at the end of the book.

George Washington's Teeth by Deborah Chandra and Madeleine Comora. Farrar, Straus and Giroux, 2003. 2–6. Relates biographical facts about the president's presidency in a conversational manner while sharing the trials and tribulations of his terrible dental problems.

Lincoln: A Photobiography by Russell Freedman. Clarion Books, 1987. 5–6. Authentic photographs, letters, posters, etc., enrich the fact-filled text detailing his life from birth to death.

Lives of the Presidents: Fame, Shame (and What the Neighbors Thought) by Kathleen Krull. Harcourt, 1998. 3–6. Instead of the usual presidential biography collection, this focuses on presidential strengths, weaknesses, hobbies, food, fashion, etc., that made them famous or shameful.

The President of the United States by Scott Ingram. Blackbirch Press, 2002. K–3. Expository text of the role of the president from eligibility to campaign, then election. Covers facts, reactions in crisis situations and other basic issues of the presidency.

So You Want to Be President? by Judith St. George. Philomel Books, 2000. 3–6. Compares and contrasts various facts about the presidents such as previous jobs, how many lived in log cabins, who had college educations, how they felt about being president, etc. Caldecott Medal, 2001.

Professional/Reference Resources

Library Sparks, October 2004, Vol. 2, No. 2.

> "So Many Books ... So Little Time" by Kathleen T. Horning, pages 2–3.

> "Meet the Illustrator: David Small" by TeachingBooks.net, pages 16–21.

> "Paired Readings: Fiction & Nonfiction, Partner with David Small" by Pat Miller, pages 27–31.

> "Vote for Book Clubs" by Laura J. H. Smith, pages 32–35.

> "Campaign Slogans," page 47.

> "Presidential Nicknames," page 48.

The Mailbox Intermediate: The Idea Magazine for Teachers, Sept. 2004. Vol. 26, No. 4

Presidents of the U.S. Fact Cards. Toucan Valley Publications, 2001. A binder with 44 cards filled with facts about each president's character and the life he led from birth to grave. Includes presidents still alive through 2001.

Multimedia

Abraham Lincoln. Nest Entertainment, Inc., 1993. VHS, DVD. 1–5. Animated format detailing the trials and tribulations of Lincoln as president. One in a series of famous Americans. (VHS requires purchase of separate cassettes for English and Spanish, DVD format includes both.)

Patriotic Songs & Marches by Dennis Buck. Kimbo Educational, 1991. CD. PreK–5. Lyrics and melody for some of the songs, others like "Hail to the Chief" are instrumentals. Excellent selection of songs to complement social studies lessons.

So You Want to Be President? Scholastic/Weston Woods, 2002. VHS.

Web Sites

HyperDictionary
hyperdictionary.com/dictionary/character+assassination

Merriam-Webster
wordcentral.com

Suzy Red
www.suzyred.com/quotes.html

The White House
www.whitehouse.gov/history/presidents/index.html

Yahooligans! Reference: Thesaurus
yahooligans.yahoo.com/reference/thesaurus

Yahooligans! The Web Guide for Kids
yahooligans.yahoo.com/reference/wak/presidents/index.html

Collaboration Notes

SPOTLIGHT ON THE

CANDIDATE

© 2005 by Aileen Kirkham (UpstartBooks)

Interview Cards

Enlarge to desired size.

Who gave you the idea
to run for president?

What was the first question
Booger Boy asked you to
make you look stupid in
front of your friends when
you said you'd run for
president?

Question 1:
U.S. Kids Magazine

Question 2:
Highlights Magazine

© 2005 by Aileen Kirkham (UpstartBooks)

What were his other two questions about?

How many names did you have to have on your petition to get your name on the presidential ballot?

Question 3:
CNN TV News

Question 4:
FOX TV News

How did your girlfriend Abby act when she found out you were running for president?

What did Lane say his job was up to Election Day?

Question 5:

New York Times Newspaper

Question 6:

www.yahooligans.com

© 2005 by Aileen Kirkham (UpstartBooks)

Question 7:
www.worldbook.com

Why did Lane say that the old lady you chose for vice president would help you get more votes?

Question 8:
Boys Life Magazine

Why didn't you pick Abby for your first lady?

© 2005 by Aileen Kirkham (UpstartBooks)

What was Lane's plan for getting over 20 million dollars to run your campaign?

What promise did you make to the kids at school if they elected you president, and why do you think it upset Booger Boy and the principal?

Question 9:
American Girl

Question 10:

© 2005 by Aileen Kirkham (UpstartBooks)

Interview Card Answers

(To refresh your memory from year to year.)

1. My friend Lane and I were playing pool while the grown-ups watched the presidential conventions. He said a kid should be president, but he couldn't run because people didn't want a smart president, but one that made them feel good. He said I could be president, and he could help me do it. *(pages 3 and 4)*

2. He asked if I knew about the presidency and who would be next in line to be president if the president and the vice-president died. I told him Arnold Schwarzenegger. *(page 13)*

3. His next two questions were as president, what do you have to do to declare war, and what's the electoral college? Since my friends were laughing about the first answer, I wanted to keep 'em laughing so I said the first step to declare war would be to call CNN to bring the cameras. As for the electoral college, I made him even madder when I said it was a school to learn how to be an electrician. *(page 13)*

4. After a week of badgering every grown-up Lane and I saw, we got the 2,000 signatures required by the state of Wisconsin to be on the ballot. Lane sent the petition to the Division of Elections, but intentionally left out the part about me being 12 years old. *(pages 15 and 16)*

5. She said she'd missed seeing me a lot especially since Lane and I have been palling around so much. She was real happy for me and told me I'd make a great president, but when I left I saw her dabbing her eyes about something. *(pages 21–24)*

6. Lane told me that until election day, he was in charge and would tell me "what to do, what to wear, what to say and when to say it." In other words, the campaign manager is like your "spin doctor" who is very careful about making sure the voters see and know only the good things about you. *(page 27)*

7. First of all, don't call her that old lady. Her name is June Syers. She is a senior citizen, of African-American descent and is handicapped. I see her as the person who raised me because my parents were so busy working, but Lane says she'll bring in the votes from all three groups: senior citizens, African Americans and handicapped folks. *(page 31)*

8. Lane told me I should pick Chelsea instead of Abby because he thinks I need a knockout beautiful girl to get more votes. He thinks Abby looks plain, maybe even ugly. *(page 34)*

9. He called up a newspaper reporter and told the reporter that he was missing a big story if he didn't come and interview me right away. When the reporter came for the interview, he got a picture of me selling lemonade with Ms. Syers to raise campaign money. Lane said the lemonade stand wasn't really to make money, but just part of the plan to get me and my campaign in the news. *(pages 58–61)*

10. Well, in order for you to find that out (and also if I win), you'll need to read my book! *(Hold up book and give a big presidential campaign style smile!)*

ABC Bookmark Pattern

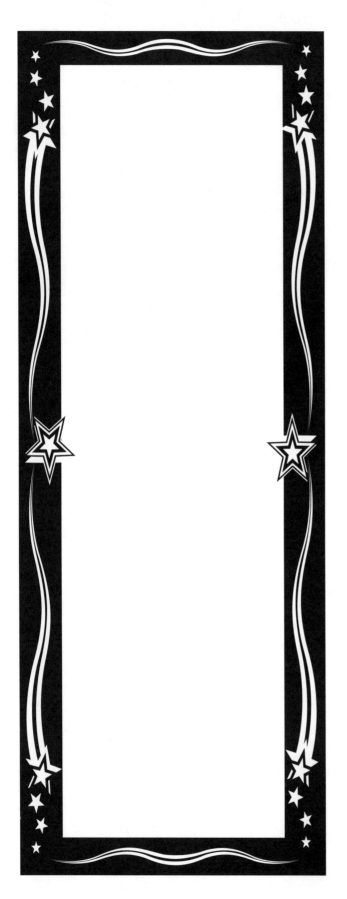
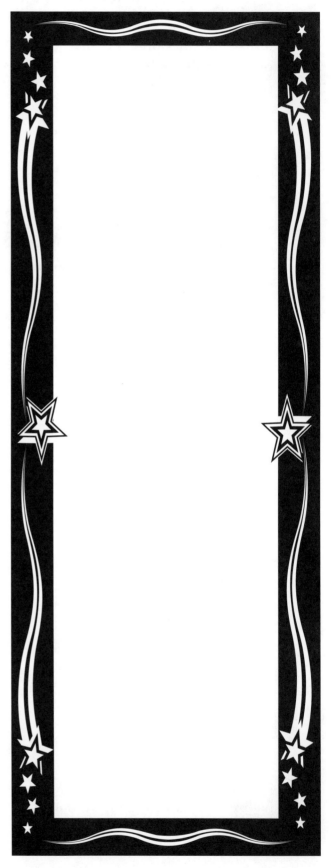

People, Places & Things Presidents

© 2005 by Aileen Kirkham (UpstartBooks)

Hall of Fame vs. Wall of Shame

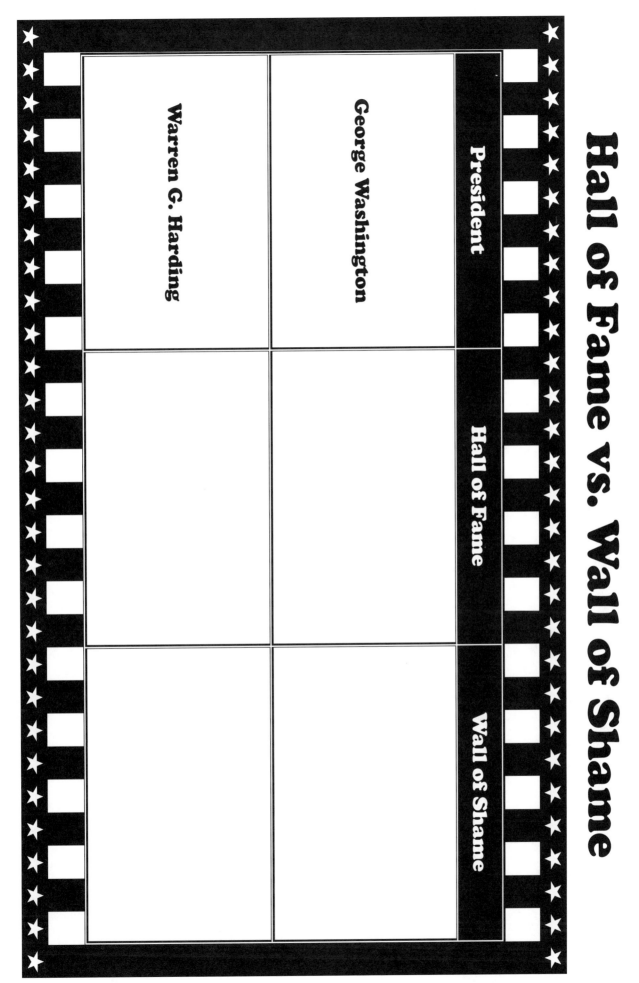

President	Hall of Fame	Wall of Shame
George Washington		
Warren G. Harding		

© 2005 by Aileen Kirkham (UpstartBooks)

Hall of Fame vs. Wall of Shame

President	Hall of Fame	Wall of Shame

© 2005 by Aileen Kirkham (UpstartBooks)

Pilgrims: Past, Present & Future

McRel Standards

History

- Understands the history of a local community and how communities in North America varied long ago.

- Understands how democratic values came to be and how they have been exemplified by people, events and symbols.

Objectives

- Define the words "pilgrim" and "pilgrimage" in broader terminology as the person(s) and the trip made for a variety of reasons: religious freedom, political freedom, desire to own land, job opportunities, divorce, death, environmental, etc.

- Use a chart to compare and contrast the pilgrims of the past, present and future by defining the who, what, when, where, why and how of specific groups.

- Use a Venn diagram to find the commonalities of pilgrims of the past, present and future.

- Use maps, globes and other geographic tools to read longitude and latitude to find specific locations.

- Read and discuss materials describing the impact of the pilgrims upon the Native American's lifestyle as written from a Native American perspective.

- Research personal family history to create a personal family tree.

- Write a report about one family member who was a pilgrim from another locale and dress a peg clothespin in the historically famous mode of dress from that time period.

Local Objectives

_____

_____

_____

_____

Rationale

Students, as contemporary pilgrims in a global society, need to gain a basic understanding of the motivations for pilgrimages of the past, present and future.

 Library Lesson
Compare and Contrast Past, Present and Future Pilgrims

Optional: Play "Coming to America," from the *Songs About America: Celebrating America's History* CD to introduce the lesson.

Display the chart from page 30. Have the students use prior knowledge to fill in the answers under the Past category as the class reviews the story of the first pilgrims of Plymouth. Share the definition of pilgrims and discuss how it is not restricted to religious pilgrimages and that it can also be synonymous with the word "immigrants." If necessary, "picture talk" a book about the first pilgrims of Plymouth, such as *William Bradford and Plymouth: A Colony Grows.* Prompt students to answer the "Who" as the group of people; the "What" as the current conditions in the country; the "When" as the time in history; the "Where" as the departure and arrival locations; the "Why" as the reason for the pilgrimage (religion, job change, divorce, death, governmental oppression, desire to own land, environmental, etc); and the "How" as the mode of transportation.

Read aloud and discuss a contemporary book of pilgrims from the bibliography such as Eve Bunting's book *How Many Days to America.* Direct students to listen for the answers to fill in the Present column on the chart as you read. Use a globe to point out a location of Cuba or another place that has had refugee type immigrants such as those in the book. Fill in the chart. Facilitate discussion with students to compare and contrast the pilgrims of the past with pilgrims of the present. Then challenge students to predict the Future category from the perspectives of pilgrims creating the first space colony.

 Bridge Activity 1
Pilgrims' AdVENNture

Using data generated from the Pilgrim Chart, compare and contrast the three types of pilgrims with an emphasis on commonalities of pilgrims throughout history and in the future. Use the Venn diagram on page 31 to make your own comparisons.

 Bridge Activity 2
Pilgrim Baseball

As a group, ask students to list basic equipment necessary to play baseball: batting helmet, ball, bat, glove, etc. Discuss how baseball can be played indoors using special equipment like globes, maps and/or atlases. Review and model the difference between longitude and latitude. Divide the class into two teams. Tell the teams that they will have three chances at bat to guess the pilgrims' country of origin. Team members must raise their hands to give the answer or their point will be given to the opposing team. Teams score a run for each correct answer. Designate a pinch hitter, such as the teacher or a classmate, for the third chance so both teams meet with success. Give two more clues if necessary to assist with success.

Pass out the baseball globe maps to all team players (see pages 32–33). Display the clues one by one as found on the Pilgrim Baseball worksheet on page 34. **Answers:** 1. Ireland, 2. Cuba, 3. Japan, 4. Vietnam, 5. Africa, 6. Iraq.

 Bridge Activity 3
A Native American Perspective

After reading aloud a book like *Giles and Metacom: A Story of Plimoth and the Wampanoag, Squanto's Journey: The Story of the First Thanksgiving* or page 5 of *We Are the Many: A Picture Book of American Indians,* challenge students to step into the moccasins of Native Americans and generate a word bank describing their feelings when the white man arrived. Have students give their reasoning for each word.

Bridge Activity 4
It Pays to Advertise

Challenge the class to brainstorm and list as many reasons as possible for leaving America and moving to space. Divide students into groups of four or five and assign them to write commercials that would make people want to leave America and move to space. Give a specific amount of time, such as a couple of days or a week, for groups to complete and present their assignment. The commercials must:

- Last no longer than 3 minutes

- Include background music (CD) or accompaniment

- Include all members of the group in the dramatization of the commercial

- Include props and/or costuming

- Provide a written script for the teacher

Classroom Lesson
My Family Tree of History

Display, discuss and fill in a family tree pattern for yourself from the template on page 35. Then provide each student with a copy of a blank family tree. Tell the students that they need to interview family members to fill in the information. In addition to completing the family tree, direct students to research one family member who was not born in America and include the answers to the Who, What, When, Where, Why and How of being a pilgrim. They should write the answers in the form of a report to share with the class. Encourage students to bring a picture of that family member to display while giving the report.

- Who: specific relationship to student such as grandfather, great-grand-mother, etc.

- What: conditions in country they left such as bad government, no food, no medicine, etc.

- When: specific year they arrived in America

- Where: departed from what city/rural area in what country and arrived at what location in America

- Why: reason for pilgrimage such as to join other family members, new job, divorce, dangerous environment, etc.

- How: mode of transportation such as foot, train, boat, car, plane and/or a combination of these

Optional Enrichment Activity:
Clothespin Pilgrims

Provide each student with peg-style clothespins (available at Hobby Lobby, Michael's and Wal-Mart). Assign each student the task of dressing the clothespin in the clothing style that his or her family pilgrim might have worn in his or her former country. Display the clothespin with the photo while the reports are presented. Students may also wish to save the clothespins and use them as decorations on a multicultural Christmas tree for the classroom or display them on a bulletin board draped with clothesline (string). On a clothesline display you might clip the family trees, clothespin people and reports side by side.

Resources
Books

Fiction

Giles and Metacom: A Story of Plimoth and the Wampanoag by Pamela Dell. Tradition Publishing Co., 2002. 2–6. A pilgrim boy's suspicion of a Wampanoag Indian inadvertently evolves into a friendship. Layout of book offers a variety of text and illustration formats including time lines, real photos, mini-text boxes, etc.

Goodbye, Vietnam by Gloria Whelan. Random House, 1993. 3–6. Thirteen-year-old Mai's family must flee Vietnam before the government soldiers arrest and imprison her father and grandmother.

Grandfather's Journey by Allen Say. Houghton Mifflin, 1993. 2–5. The story is a flashback of grandfather moving from Japan to California. Throughout his life he travels back and forth between the two, but is forced to stay in Japan with the outbreak of World War II.

Home at Last: Sofia's Immigrant Diary (Book Two) by Kathryn Lasky. Scholastic, 2003. 2–5. A 10-year-old girl and her family transition into the Italian culture of Boston. Sophia is upset when she hears that the friend she made at Ellis Island may have to leave the U.S.

Hope in My Heart: Sofia's Immigrant Diary (Book One) by Kathryn Lasky. Scholastic, 2003. 2– 5. Ten-year-old Sofia immigrates to America, but is separated from her family and quarantined due to the misdiagnosis of an eye problem. With the help of a new friend, she survives the apathetic treatment by officials and is reunited with her family.

How Many Days to America: A Thanksgiving Story by Eve Bunting. Houghton Mifflin, 1990. 2–5. Refugees fleeing from military oppression on a Caribbean island face many dangers as boat people trying to get to a place that will offer them freedom. Upon arrival in America, they realize their experience parallels that of the Pilgrims of the first Thanksgiving.

Maggie's Door by Patricia Reilly Giff. Random House, 2003. 4–8. Nory, her brother and her mom along with friend, Sean Red Mallory, and his mom immigrate to America to leave the tragedy of the Irish potato famine. This sequel to *Nory Ryan's Song* is told in the alternating voices of Nory and Sean.

Nory Ryan's Song by Patricia Reilly Giff. Bantam Doubleday Dell, 2000. 4–8. Nory's family and her friend Sean Red Mallory's family struggle to avoid starvation and death with the onset of the Irish potato famine.

Squanto's Journey: The Story of the First Thanksgiving by Joseph Bruchac. Harcourt, 2000. 2–5. Retelling by Squanto of being kidnapped by British and sold to the Spanish to be a slave. His eventual escape to return to America directly impacted the survival of the pilgrims to build a new nation.

Thanksgiving on Thursday by Mary Pope Osborne. Random House, 2002. 2–5. Jack and Annie use their Magic Tree House to time travel to the 1600s and visit with the Pilgrims and the Wampanoag Indians during the celebration of the first Thanksgiving.

Nonfiction

Coming to America: The Story of Immigration by Betsy Maestro. Scholastic, 1996. 2–5. Tells a simplified history of America's immigrants beginning with Native Americans to contemporary immigrants of today.

Don't Know Much About the Pilgrims by Kenneth C. Davis. HarperCollins, 2002. 2–6. Questions and answers about the Pilgrims plus maps, recipes, clothing styles and other fascinating Pilgrim trivia.

Eating the Plates: A Pilgrim Book of Food and Manners by Lucille Recht Penner. Simon & Schuster, 1991. 2–6. Manners, customs and habits necessary for the cultural and physical survival of the pilgrims.

The First Thanksgiving by Susan Whitehurst. PowerKids Press, 2002. 2–5. Page layout includes mixed format of mini-text boxes, authentic pictures and artists' renderings of the first Thanksgiving. Web sites are listed, too.

If You Sailed on the Mayflower in 1620 by Ann McGovern. Scholastic, 1991. 2–5. Question and answer format of the experience of the people first called pilgrims, includes a detailed cutaway drawing of the Mayflower.

Immigrant Kids by Russell Freedman. Penguin Putnam, 1980. 3–6. Documents the living and working conditions of immigrant children in the U.S. in the early 1900s.

A Kid's Guide to African American History by Nancy I. Sanders. Chicago Review Press,

2000. 3–6. Time line of text stretches from days of pre-slavery to contemporary times in America. Includes games, crafts, stories, songs, recipes, Web sites, etc.

Kurdish Family by Karen O'Connor. Lerner Publishing Group, 1996. 3–6. Details the true story of a Kurdish family being persecuted in Northern Iraq, and their trip to escape to the U.S. to start a new life.

The Mayflower by Susan Whitehurst. PowerKids Press, 2003. 2–5. Page layout includes mixed format of mini-text boxes, authentic pictures and artists' renderings of life on the Mayflower. Web sites are listed, too.

N. C. Wyeth's Pilgrims by Robert San Souci. Chronicle Books, 1991. 2–5. Retells the story of the pilgrims.

The Pilgrims Before the Mayflower by Susan Whitehurst. PowerKids Press, 2002. 2–5. Historical background of first pilgrims prior to Mayflower voyage.

A Plymouth Partnership: Pilgrims and Native Americans by Susan Whitehurst. PowerKids Press, 2002. 2–5. Page layout includes mixed format of mini-text boxes, authentic pictures and artists' renderings of the pilgrim and Indian life. Web sites are included, too.

Plymouth: Surviving the First Winter by Susan Whitehurst. PowerKids Press, 2002. 2–5. Page layout includes mini-text boxes, authentic pictures and artists' renderings of this harrowing time. Web sites included.

Pushing Up the Sky: Seven Native American Plays for Children by Joseph Bruchac. Dial,

2000. 2–5. Seven traditional tales from tribes including Abenaki, Cherokee, Tlingit and Zuni. Includes ideas for props, scenery and recommended costumes.

Sarah Morton's Day: A Day in the Life of a Pilgrim Girl by Kate Waters. Scholastic, 1991. 1–4. Text and photos follow a pilgrim girl through a typical day.

Turkeys, Pilgrims, and Indian Corn: The Story of the Thanksgiving Symbols by Edna Barth. HarperCollins, 1975. 3–6. Traces historical significance of the symbols and legends of the celebration of the first Thanksgiving.

We Are the Many: A Picture Book of American Indians by Doreen Rappaport. HarperCollins, 2002. 1–5. Collective biography of American Indians dating from Tisquantum (Squanto) to contemporary times.

William Bradford and Plymouth: A Colony Grows by Susan Whitehurst. PowerKids Press, 2002. 2–6. Page layout includes mixed format of mini-text boxes, authentic pictures and artists' renderings of the pilgrims' first settlement.

Professional/Reference Resources

Library Sparks, November 2003. Vol. 1, No. 3.

"Thanksgiving Surprise Reader's Theater" by Lois Walker, pages 42–46.

Library Sparks, November 2004. Vol. 2, No. 3.

"Meet Joseph Bruchac" by Rob Reid, pages 6–9.

"Telling Tales, Sharing Lives" by Pat Miller, pages 10–14.

"Native American Heritage Month" by Diane Findlay, pages 30–36.

"Thanksgiving Mad Lib," page 48.

Multimedia

Native American Powwow (Come Celebrate With Me Series). SVE & Churchill Media, 2001. VHS. 2–5.

Songs About America: Celebrating America's History. Kimbo Educational, 2003. CD. All grades.

Stories for Thanksgiving. Scholastic/Weston Woods, 2003. VHS. 1–5.

William Bradford: First Thanksgiving (Animated Hero Classics Series). Nest Entertainment, 1992. VHS. 2–5.

Web Sites

An American Thanksgiving
www.night.net/thanksgiving
Text is kid-friendly and promotes interaction with jokes, songs, stories, games, coloring pages, certificates, poetry, etc. It even features a video game to hunt the turkey!

Kid Info
www.kidinfo.com/American_History/
Colonization_Plymouth.html

The Mayflower Society
www.mayflower.org

Pilgrim Hall Museum
www.pilgrimhall.org/museum.htm

Plimoth Plantation
www.plimoth.org

Wampanoag History
www.tolatsga.org/wampa.html

Collaboration Notes

_____

_____

_____

_____

_____

_____

_____

_____

_____

_____

_____

_____

_____

_____

_____

_____

_____

_____

_____

_____

_____

_____

Pilgrims

	Future	Present	Past
Who			
What			
When			
Where			
Why			
How			

© 2005 by Aileen Kirkham (UpstartBooks)

Pilgrims Venn Diagram

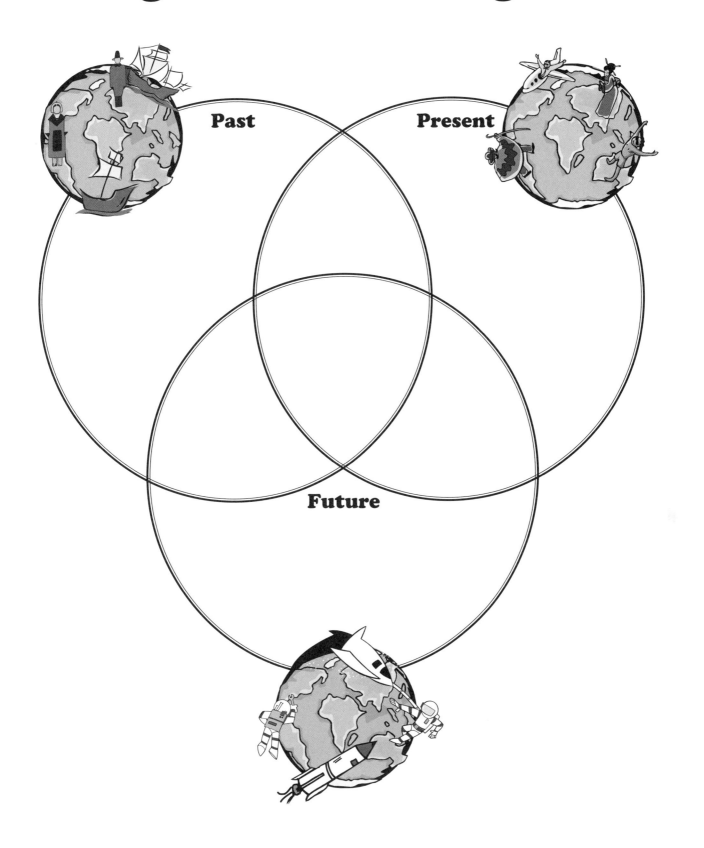

Past

Present

Future

© 2005 by Aileen Kirkham (UpstartBooks)

Pilgrim Baseball Maps

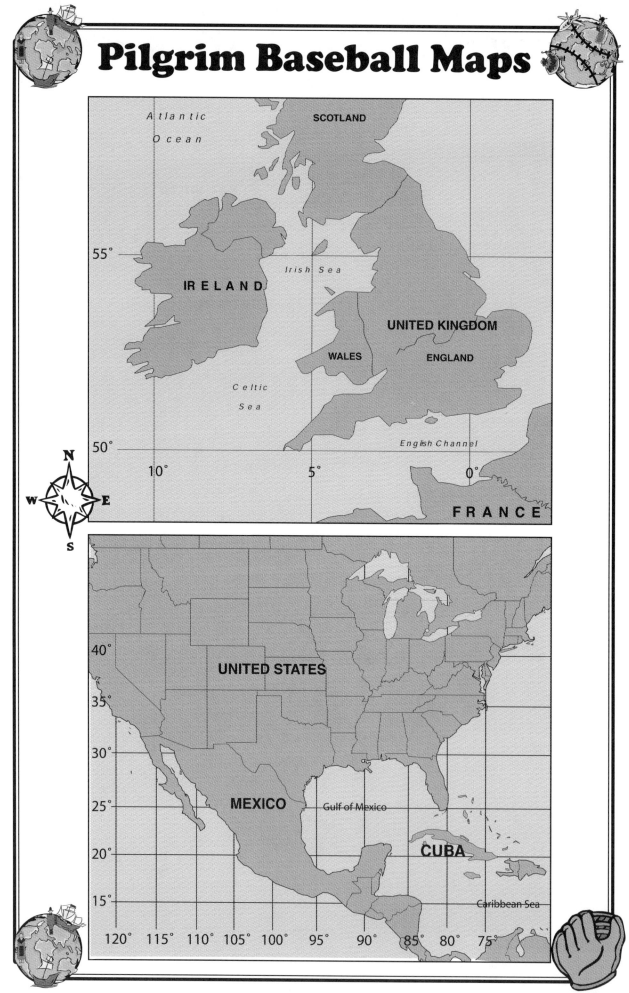

© 2005 by Aileen Kirkham (UpstartBooks)

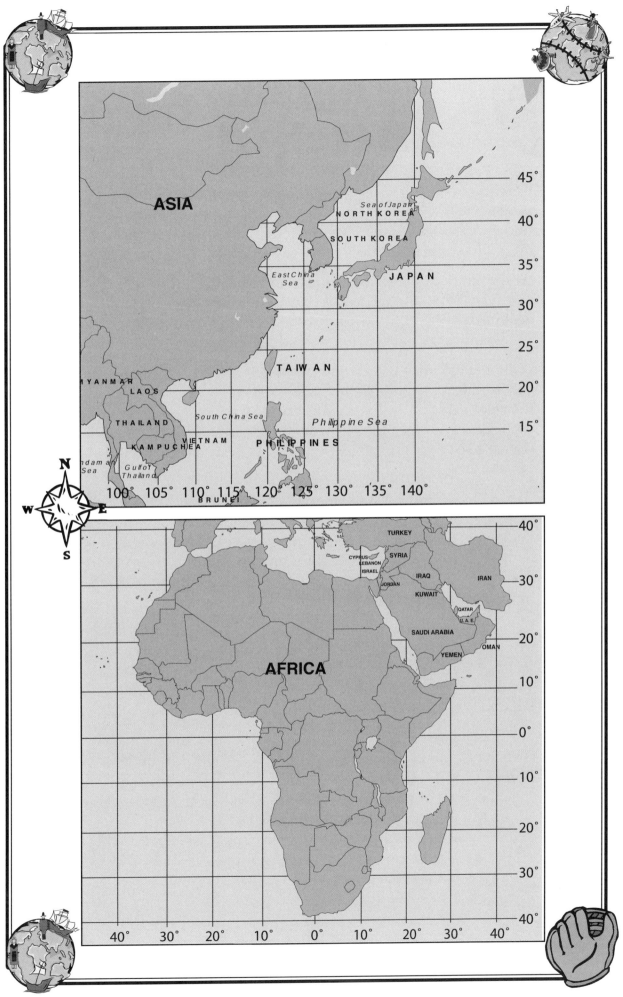

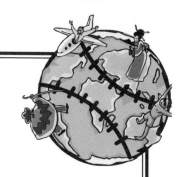

Pilgrim Baseball

1. We left from this European island country at longitude 10 degrees west and latitude 55 degrees north because of a potato famine. Our story is told in *Nory Ryan's Song*. Two more clues are: it's called the Emerald Isle and it is home to the legend of St. Patrick. What is it?

2. We left this North American island country at longitude 75 degrees west and latitude 20 degrees north. We were boat people like those described in *How Many Days to America*. Two more clues are that it's famous for cigars and is a short distance from Florida.

3. I left from this Asian island country at longitude 135 degrees east and latitude 35 degrees north because my family wished to move to California. My story is told in the Caldecott winning book, *Grandfather's Journey*. Two more clues would be that it is the country that attacked Pearl Harbor on December 7, 1941, and made sushi a popular food. What is it?

4. We left this southeast Asian country at longitude 105 degrees east and latitude 20 degrees north. Our story, *Goodbye, Vietnam*, will tell you that the soldiers were coming to arrest my father and grandmother to put them in jail so we escaped by boat to Hong Kong. Two more clues are that American soldiers fought a war there in the 1960s and 1970s and the country's name is in the title of our book. What is it?

5. We left this island continent at longitude 25 degrees east and latitude 0 degrees as unwilling pilgrims forced to make a voyage by white slave traders. Our story is told in *A Kid's Guide to African American History*. Two more clues are that many things from this land like the title of the book and African grey parrots have the name of the continent as part of the word in the description. What is it?

6. We left this country at longitude 45 degrees east and latitude 30 degrees north to escape the cruel leader, Saddam Hussein, who wanted to kill us. Our story is told in *Kurdish Family*. Two more clues are that former President George Bush Sr. and his son, President George W. Bush, have sent soldiers to fight against this country's soldiers and hope to have all of the people in this country enjoy freedom. What is it?

© 2005 by Aileen Kirkham (UpstartBooks)

Family Tree

© 2005 by Aileen Kirkham (UpstartBooks)

Unit 3

Hurricanes: Past, Present & Protection

McRel Standards

History

- Understands major discoveries in science and technology, some of their social and economic effects and the major scientists and inventors responsible for them.

Science

Earth Science

- Understands atmospheric processes and the water cycle.

Physical Science

- Understands the structure and properties of matter.

- Understands the sources and properties of energy.

- Understands forces and motion.

Nature of Science

- Understands the nature of scientific inquiry.

- Understands the scientific enterprise.

Objectives

- Connect the concept of a hurricane as a weather system via experiences and ideas while speaking, listening, viewing and participating in hands-on activities.

- Use a web to define a hurricane, its formation, dynamics and categories.

- Name the two worst storms to ever hit the mainland U.S. in relation to the loss of life and property damage. (Galveston Hurricane of 1900 and Hurricane Andrew).

- Research the qualifications and responsibilities of a meteorologist.

- Develop a list of safety measures for protection from a hurricane.

- Set up a student weather station to collect, analyze and report on current weather conditions.

Local Objectives

_____

_____

_____

_____

Rationale

Students, as current and/or future travelers in a global society, need to gain a basic understanding of the weather conditions of hurricanes and their impact on weather forecasting and safety measures to protect the world populations.

Library Lesson
Inside Hurricanes—Take Cover!

Divide the students into five groups and assign each group a sound. Model one sound at a time and direct actions as a conductor conducts music so students know when to stop noisemaking for discussion.

- Rain: group tapping fingernails on desktops

- Hail: group tapping knuckles on desktops

- Thunder: group hitting tables with flat palms of hands

- Wind: whistling or howling voice

- Tornado: arms and hands swirling from above desk to desktop while roaring with voice

Ask the students what these noises might be a part of and call on students to guess until someone guesses weather. Then ask what kind of weather. If they say thunderstorm, tell them that it is worse, but it includes thunderstorms. If they guess tornadoes, tell them it is worse and includes tornadoes. Have the students keep guessing until they conclude that it is a hurricane. Read aloud *The Magic School Bus Inside a Hurricane*. Direct students to listen carefully and to be ready to answer the following questions to fill in a web about a hurricane.

1. What is one of the major birthplaces of a hurricane?

2. What is the difference between a tropical storm and a hurricane?

3. Why are hurricanes given names?

4. What is the atmospheric weather recipe for a hurricane?

5. What part of a hurricane has no wind?

6. What is the dome of water called that is part of a hurricane and results in flooding?

7. Where did a hurricane hit the U.S. mainland in 1900 and have the highest death toll of at least 6,000 people, possibly as high as 12,000?

8. What has dramatically decreased the number of deaths in hurricanes?

9. List three bad things that hurricanes do.

10. List three good things that hurricanes do.

11. What word that starts with "m" is the title of the person who sends official weather forecasts to TV and radio stations?

12. List as many safety measures as you can that help protect people and property from a hurricane.

Using the web template on page 44 or an Inspiration software Web template, solicit and map the answers from students regarding the questions about hurricanes.

Bridge Activity 1
Meet a Meteorologist

As a group, discuss and brainstorm the educational qualifications, expertise and responsibilities of a meteorologist. Verify your answers by reading a book about a meteorologist, inviting a meteorologist to your school to do a presentation, scheduling a field trip to visit a meteorologist at a TV station and/or visiting the Web site www.weatherwizkids.com/careercorner. htm. Add information links to circle 11 on the Hurricane Web.

Bridge Activity 2
Weather Forecasting Technology

Show the video *Inventions for Students: Computerized Weather Forecasting & Firefighting*. Then discuss the futuristic possibilities of protection from bad weather such as hurricanes.

Bridge Activity 3
Student Weather Station

View and discuss the video *All About Meteorology*. List the weather instruments that can be acquired and easily utilized at school. Collect the instruments and set up a student weather station to chart the weather data for a week.

Bridge Activity 4
Hurricane Protection

Discuss statistical probabilities of hurricanes in your local area, noting that even if hurricanes hit coastal areas, they can impact weather surrounding them up to 600 miles or more. If there's a high probability of a direct hit in your local area, have a class discussion to generate an exact list of safety measures. Be sure to include:

- Supplies—batteries for flashlight, radios and/or laptop computers; food; water; clothing; medications and first aid kits; pet relocation plans; etc.

- Highway Signage for Evacuation Routes

Add information links to circle 12 on the Hurricane Web.

Classroom Lesson
Hurricanes in 3D

Visit www.miamisci.org/hurricane to gather and prepare the materials needed for the lesson. Click on Inside a Hurricane, then click on Andrew in 3D (a printable pattern for students to make 3D glasses to view Hurricane Andrew's image complete with its eye) and Make a Hurricane Spiral (a printable pattern for students to make a graphic model of a hurricane spiral that actually moves).

Divide the students into five groups and assign them the hurricane action sound for their group. Review how to make each sound and practice with one group at a time. Again, remember to direct actions as a conductor conducts music so students know when to stop noisemaking for discussion and lesson.

- Rain: group tapping fingernails on desktops

- Hail: group tapping knuckles on desktops

- Thunder: group hitting tables with flat palms of hands

- Wind: whistling or howling voice

- Tornado: arms and hands swirling from above desk to desktop while roaring with voice

Read the information about the following items in *Hurricanes* by Seymour Simon:

- the 1900 Galveston, Texas, hurricane

- the Safir-Simpson Hurricane Scale of hurricane categories

- Hurricane Andrew

- the next to the last page that lists what to do after a hurricane passes by

Make note of the fact that the 1900 hurricane of Galveston had the worst death toll of any hurricane to ever hit the U.S. mainland while Hurricane Andrew holds the record for the worst property loss. Query students as to what category these storms were.

Access the Web site www.miamisci.org/hurricane. Click on Inside a Hurricane, then click on Andrew in 3D. Share with students that they will have the opportunity to make 3D glasses and experience a hurricane much like a storm tracker plane crew would. Model how to make the glasses, pass out materials and assist students with making the glasses. Stay at the same Web site and click on Make a Hurricane Spiral. Demonstrate how to make the model and provide students with materials to make their individual models.

To review hurricanes, view and discuss the video *Ever-Changing Earth for Students: Hurricane.* Add any information links from the video to the Hurricane Web.

 **Resources**
Books

Fiction

Annie's Storm by Beverly Hirsch. Cardinal Enterprises of Florida, 1999. K–3. Facing an impending hurricane, a young girl worries about herself, her family and her friend, Mrs. Mockingbird.

Galveston's Summer of the Storm by Julie Lake. TCU Press, 2003. 3–6. From a girl's perspective, this book gives a terrifying account of living through the horrendous hurricane that actually hit Galveston, Texas, in 1900.

The Great Storm: The Hurricane Diary of J. T. King by Lisa Waller Rogers. Texas Tech University Press, 2002. 3–6. The frightening events detailed in a boy's diary based on the factual events of the devastating hurricane that hit Galveston, Texas, in 1900.

Hurricane! by Pat Lakin. Lerner Publishing Group, 2000. K–3. Instead of enjoying their cottage and its beach location, a young girl's family must make preparations for the landfall of Hurricane Bob. The family experiences the storm while at the cottage and must make repairs from the storm's damage. At the end of the book a list of questions is provided that kids might ask (which can provide a springboard to discussion of hurricanes and the safety measures necessary for protection).

Hurricane! by Jonathan London. HarperCollins, 1998. K–3. One minute the two Puerto Rican boys are snorkeling on the reef near their home, the next they are joining their neighbors to race for a shelter. After the storm, they are relieved to find that the storm has left minimal damage.

Hurricane by David Wiesner. Clarion Books, 1990. K–4. In the aftermath of a hurricane, two boys discover that an uprooted tree becomes a magic carpet to any adventure on which their imaginations can take them.

Hurricane Mystery by Gertrude Chandler Warner. Albert Whitman, 1996. 3–6. The Boxcar Children visit a family friend living off the coast of South Carolina. They find themselves committed to finding out why strange things are happening as rumors circulate of a pirate treasure buried nearby.

The Magic School Bus Inside a Hurricane by Joanna Cole and Bruce Degen. Scholastic, 1995. 3–6. En route to the weather station to collect information for the class weather projects, the bus is transformed into a plane that flies into a hurricane. As the bus/plane swirls and rocks, Ms. Frizzle shares the facts of hurricane formation and movement.

Sergio and the Hurricane by Alexandra Wallner. Henry Holt & Company, 2000. K–3. At first the young Puerto Rican boy, Sergio, is thrilled with the excitement of an approaching hurricane, but those feelings change when he experiences the storm firsthand and realizes how fortunate he is that the grown-ups of the town were prepared for the storm.

The Silent Storm by Sherry Garland. Harcourt, 1995. 4–7. Having witnessed the death of her parents in a previous hurricane (which resulted in her becoming mute), 13-year-old Alyssa must face another hurricane while living with her grandmother.

Tragedy from the Sea: The Galveston Hurricane of 1900 by Bonnie Highsmith Taylor. Perfection Learning, 2002. 3–6. Neighbors join with Vernon and his family to recover from the 1900 Galveston Hurricane.

The Truth About Sparrows by Marian Hale. Henry Holt & Company, 2004. 5–8. Drought stricken Missouri forces 12-year-old Sadie's family to move to Texas to make a new home and find new friends. An incoming hurricane brings more trauma to the family.

Nonfiction

Do Tornadoes Really Twist? Questions and Answers About Tornadoes and Hurricanes by Melvin and Gilda Berger. Scholastic, 2000. 3–6. Answers various questions about two of some of the most violent and destructive storms on Earth including their duration, locales, weather forecasting capabilities, safety measures, etc.

Howling Hurricanes by Louise Spilsbury. Heinemann Library, 2004. 3–6. Includes answers to questions about hurricane dynamics, their history, forecasting them and the possibility of predicting them in the future.

Hurricanes by Catherine Chambers. Heinemann Library, 2000. 3–8. Includes all the elements of a hurricane and the impact on people and landforms. Also examines the phenomenon of global warming and how it may impact weather systems such as El Niño, which generates violent hurricanes.

Hurricanes by Seymour Simon. HarperCollins, 2003. 3–7. Explains where and how hurricanes take form, the categorical rankings for destruction and the safety measures one should take prior to and during impact. Photographs of actual hurricane sites and computer-generated graphics greatly enhance text.

Hurricanes: Earth's Biggest Storms by Patricia Lauber. Scholastic, 1996. 3–6. Using photographs, maps and diagrams of some of this century's worst hurricanes, this book shares the hypnotic and horrific elements of hurricanes.

Storms and Hurricanes by Kathy Gemmell. EDC Publishing, 1996. 3–7. Examines weather patterns of storms ranging from sandstorms to hurricanes; the science of predicting and forecasting storms; and the techniques for reducing the effects of their powerful destructive forces.

Weather Math by Kieran Walsh. Rourke Publishing LLC, 2004. 4–7. Connects the scientific scales of measurement for the intensity of storms with mathematical equations while underscoring the importance of studying math as a necessity for becoming a meteorologist.

Wild Weather: Hurricanes! by Lorraine Jean Hopping. Scholastic, 1995. 2–4. Discusses formation, degrees of destruction depending on intensity, weather forecasting, safety tips, etc.

Professional/Reference

A Guide for Using the Magic School Bus Inside a Hurricane in the Classroom by Greg Young. Teacher Created Materials, 1996. Provides pre- and post-reading activities, lessons, a unit assessment tool, an annotated bibliography, etc.

Isaac's Storm: A Man, A Time, and the Deadliest Storm in History by Erik Larson. Vintage Books, 1999. Details historic roots of the U.S. weather service and how its rocky beginnings influenced Isaac Cline, the head weather scientist in Galveston, to ignore the ominous weather conditions in 1900 that prefaced the worst hurricane to ever hit the mainland U.S. Also includes an interesting parallel between Isaac and his brother, who disputed Isaac's attitude toward the approaching storm, and led to the estrangement of the two brothers. Photos of the devastation to Galveston and its rebuilding process are also included.

Multimedia

All About Meteorology. Schlessinger Media, 2000. VHS. K–4.

Ever-Changing Earth for Students: Hurricane. Discovery Communications/SVE, Inc., 2004. VHS. 1–6.

Inventions for Students: Computerized Weather Forecasting & Firefighting. Discovery Communications, Inc./Clearvue & SVE, 2004. DVD, VHS. 4–6.

Web Sites

Canadian Hurricane Centre Just for Kids! www.ns.ec.gc.ca/weather/hurricane/kids.html

Howstuffworks www.science.howstuffworks.com/hurricane.html

Miami Museum of Science & Planetarium
www.miamisci.org/hurricane

National Geographic.com Kids—Flying Into the Eye of a Hurricane
www.nationalgeographic.com/ngkids/0308/hurricane

National Oceanic and Atmospheric Administration
hurricanes.noaa.gov/index.html

Scholastic—Hurricanes
teacher.scholastic.com/activities/wwatch/hurricanes/index.htm

Weather Wiz Kids
www.weatherwizkids.com/careercorner.htm

Collaboration Notes

Hurricane Web

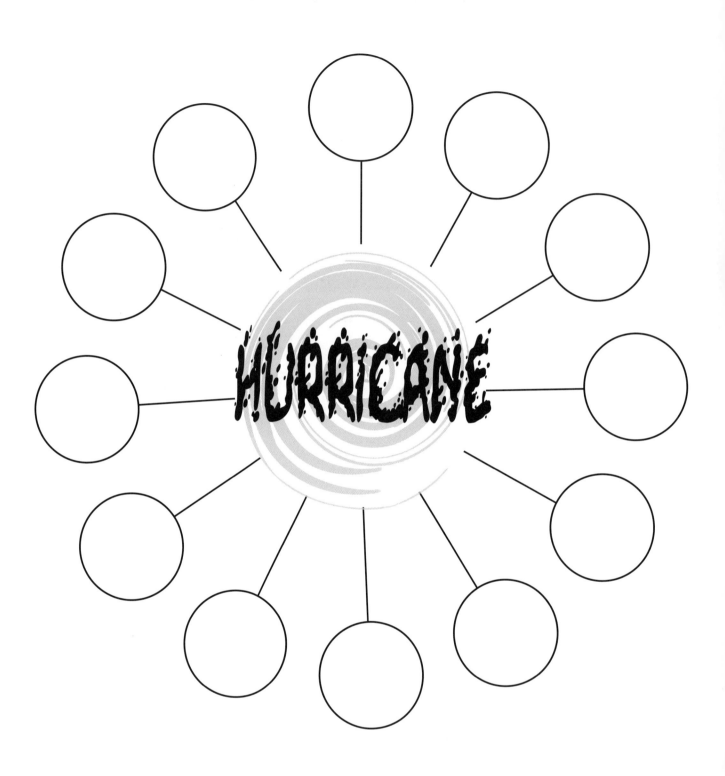

 © 2005 by Aileen Kirkham (UpstartBooks)

Inventive Minds: Past, Present & Future

McRel Standards

Economics

- Understands that scarcity of productive resources requires choices that generate opportunity costs.

- Understands characteristics of different economic systems, economic institutions and economic incentives.

- Understands the concept of prices and the interaction of supply and demand in a market economy.

Science

Physical Science

- Understands the structure and properties of matter.

- Understands the sources of property of energy.

- Understands forces and motion.

Nature of Science

- Understands the nature of scientific inquiry.

- Understands the scientific enterprise.

Objectives

- Use cause and effect logic to understand the motivations of an inventor.

- Explore inventors and their inventions to understand their impact upon society.

- Research an invention and generate a web to show how it has radiated into other applications.

- Define and implement the word "modification" in relation to inventions.

- Create an original invention and/or one using a Web site's instructions.

- Discern the difference between fact and opinion.

Local Objectives

_____

_____

_____

_____

Rationale

Students, as current and/or future inventors in a global society, need to understand that:

- Human need and creativity are the driving forces of inventive minds

- Being an inventor does not guarantee financial success and happiness

- Inventions generate new technologies

- New technologies generate new jobs

Library Lesson
The Real McCoy

Hold up *Where the Sidewalk Ends* and an electrical cord/cable. Comment on the convenience and innovative idea of the Post-it® note that you have used to mark pages 48 and 49. Read aloud the poem "Inventions" and use the cord as a prop to dramatize the poem. If the book *Mistakes that Worked* is available, read aloud the origin of Post-it notes on page 51.

Display *The Real McCoy: The Life of an African-American Inventor* and ask students about the meaning of the idiomatic phrase "the Real McCoy." Hold up a box of Nabisco Nilla® Wafers and a grocery store generic brand. Ask kids which one would be considered the best of the best and why. (Answer: The Nabisco Nilla Wafers would be the Real McCoy, meaning the original best, while grocery store cookies are a copy of the tasty bestseller.) Display the questions below. Read the book aloud, then discuss the questions.

1. Why did he invent the oil cup? (*He was motivated by his job on the railroad.*)

2. Why was it difficult to get a good job and sell his ideas? (*He lived in a racist society.*)

3. What idiom did railroad people use when wanting to purchase his invention instead of a copy of it? (*Real McCoy.*)

4. What is the family tree history of his first invention, in other words, is his invention still in use today? If so, use a webbing graphic to reinforce the concept that inventions radiate into other applications.

Bridge Activity 1
Inventions Challenge

Prepare the class to play the Inventions Challenge game, similar to Family Feud. Divide the group into two teams. Have one teammate from each team leave the area or be out of listening distance while you query the teams on the most important inventions in current society. Elicit the top six inventions they have used in their lifetimes, three from each team. Have the students cover their eyes, then have each team vote on the top six inventions. Count and record votes on a piece of paper. Call back one team representative at a time to try to match his or her team's answers. Ask the students if it matters if the contestant matches. (It doesn't matter because it's not fact, just peoples' opinions.) The most important thing about this game is to understand the impact of these inventions to improve the quality of life.

Bridge Activity 2
Name That Invention

Go to the Web site, www.inventivekids.com/indexFlash.html and click on Name That Invention. Each time a question is given, players are to choose from the pictures and click on the one that they believe answers the question. When the correct answer is selected, there is happy music and a message of congratulations. When the incorrect answer is given, players are given a chance to try again. The bonus of playing is that with each correct answer, there is a blurb of information about the inventor and the origins of the invention. If more competitive/interactive play is desired, divide the class into teams, then use a Tic-Tac-Toe format to earn X's or O's as the teams select the correct answers. It is recommended that you have an extra question ready to even the score so that the teams end in a tie. Remind students that everyone's a winner since the object of the game is to learn about inventors and inventions.

Bridge Activity 3
Inventive World

Go to the Web site, www.inventivekids.com/indexFlash.html and click on the Inventive World link. This link is an interactive virtual reality Star Trek-type space mission in which decisions are made that can make or break the success of the mission. Reference that NASA uses a similar, but much more sophisticated simulation module to train future astronauts. If students are mature enough, view and discuss clips from the movie *Apollo 13* as an enrichment activity.

Bridge Activity 4
Keep Your Eyes Open

Go to the Web site www.inventivekids.com/indexFlash.html and click on the Keep Your Eyes Open link. This link is a Concentration-type game—an interactive activity that challenges the players to match two pictures. If a match isn't made, the next player gets to take a turn. When a match is made, the inventor and the invention's history are displayed to explain the picture. To make this more challenging, divide the class into two teams and keep score. It is recommended that you have an extra question ready to even the score so that the teams end in a tie. The object of the game is to learn about inventors and inventions.

Classroom Lesson
Scientific Inquiry & Enterprise

Have the class view *Inventions for Students: Helpful Inventions*. Discuss inspirations for innovations in the DVD and whether or not they're new ideas or modifications.

Go to the Web site inventors.about.com/library/inventors/blbandaid.htm and click on the Band-Aid® Time line link. Display and discuss the use of the most recent types of Band-Aids listed in the time line. Reference the time line as you show them to the class. Define the word "modifications" and generate a list of what motivated the modifications in the Band-Aid over the years: more effective, less messy, more cost-effective, etc.

Divide the class into groups. Direct each group to select a category from which they wish to invent something new or modify something that has already been invented. Explain that this is the beginning of the process for scientific inquiry and enterprise as inventors. The categories are:

- Telecommunication
- Transportation
- Health and Safety
- Recreation
- Pets

The presentation may be in any type of format including a Power Point presentation, skit, overhead projector presentation with visual aids like posters or models, videos, etc. As a group they are to use specific criteria in preparation for the presentation to the class, which must include:

1. Name of the Invention/Creation = 5 points

2. Name of the Inventors/Designers = 5 points

3. An in-depth explanation of the cause and effect logic for the idea of the invention/creation, a visual graphic/diagram and why it is a worthwhile invention: less messy, easier to use, more cost-effective, etc. = 80 points

4. Targeted Population for Purchase: adults, children, boys and/or girls, etc. = 5 points.

5. Create and display a web if this invention/creation has applications in more than one of the five categories.

 **Resources**
Books

Fiction

The Gadget War by Betsy Duffey. Puffin Books, 1991. 3–6. Third grader Kelly is the inventor of 43 inventions, but meets Albert who is determined to beat her record and prove that he's the king of gadget inventions.

Hey Kid, Want to Buy a Bridge? by Jon Scieszka. Viking, 2002. 3–6. With the help of a magical book, Fred, Sam and Joe accidentally travel through time to New York City in 1877. Inventive minds of their ancestors must help them find their way back.

The Midnight Mystery by Gertrude Chandler Warner. Whitman & Co., 2003. 3–6. A renowned inventor of one-of-a-kind clocks is threatened with trouble at home until

Benny, Jessie, Violet and Henry investigate to find the culprit.

Nonfiction

Accidents May Happen by Charlotte Foltz Jones. Bantam Doubleday Dell, 1996. 3–6. Explains a broad spectrum of how things came to be such as dynamite, anesthesia, the national anthem, etc. Also includes an index and bibliographical references.

The Amazing Mr. Franklin or The Boy Who Read Everything by Ruth Ashby. Peachtree Publishers, 2004. 3–6. Details astounding achievements including the inventions of one of American's most famous historical figures.

Benjamin Franklin: Early American Genius by Maya Glass. Rosen Publishing Group, 2003. 3–6. Details the life of this great man from struggling apprentice to fame as a printer, politician and inventor.

Clarence Birdseye by Tiffany Peterson. Heinemann Library, 2003. 3–6. Recounts the story of inventing the process to flash-freeze food to maintain flavor, be frozen for periods of time and the founding of Birds Eye Frosted Foods in 1929.

The Computer by Gayle Worland. Capstone Press, 2003. 3–6. Historical time line of this invention from gargantuan main frames to personal computers. Also features an index and bibliographical references.

Dr. Knowledge Presents Strange & Fascinating Facts About Famous Brands by Charles Reichblum. Workman Publishing, 2004. Young Adult. Historical information about name brands, their logos, factual events, etc.

Eureka! Poems About Inventors by Joyce Sidman. Lerner Publishing Group, 2002. 3–6. From famous to obscure inventors of long ago to current times, this author shares their stories in verse.

The Genius of Leonardo rewritten by Guido Visconti. Barefoot Books, 2000. 3–6. Details the inventions, dreams and life's work of Leonardo from the perspective of his young assistant, Giacomo. This translation is a picture book biography with a mixture of fiction about the assistant and fact about Leonardo's work.

George Eastman by Jennifer Blizin Gillis. Heinemann Library, 2004. 3–6. Provides significant details of the founder of Kodak who invented the method of using rolls of film instead of plates to take photos. Also includes an index and bibliographical references.

Great Discoveries & Inventions that Advanced Industry and Technology by Antonio Casanellas. Gareth Stevens, 2000. 3–6. Translated from a book published in Barcelona, Spain, are various inventions, their function and the process of creating them.

Imaginative Inventions: The Who, What, Where, When, and Why of Roller Skates, Potato Chips, Marbles, and Pie and More! by Charise Mericle Harper. Little, Brown and Company, 2001. K–3.

Inventors and Inventions in Colonial America by Charlie Samuel. PowerKids Press, 2002. 3–6. Details a who's who of inventors and inventions from this time period including Benjamin Franklin, David Rittenhouse, Benjamin Banneker, etc.

John Deere by Margaret Hall. Heinemann Library, 2004. 3–6. From his early years to the manufacturing of farm equipment that is sold today, this biography of John Deere underscores his continued importance to modern society.

The Kids' Invention Book by Arlene Erlbach. Lerner Publishing Group, 1996. A step-by-step guide to being a young inventor that covers everything from contests to 11 stories of real kids who are inventors.

The Light Bulb by Marc Tyler Nobleman. Capstone Press, 2003. 3–6. Narrative of the first invention of the light bulb to its currents uses and the inventor who made it all happen. Includes an index and bibliographical references.

Milton Bradley by Raymond H. Miller. Thomson Gale, 2004. 3–6. Life story of the founder of the Milton Bradley Company and the games developed by him and his company, many of which are still popular today.

Mistakes that Worked by Charlotte Foltz Jones. Bantam Doubleday Dell, 1991. K–5. Details 40 items that were invented by accident including Post-its®, Velcro®, Silly Putty®, etc.

The Real McCoy: The Life of an African-American Inventor by Wendy Towle. Scholastic, 1992. 3–6. Born in Canada, having an engineering degree from Scotland, this man was never given the recognition due to him because of his race. One of his inventions, the oil cup, has been modified and is in use today on the space shuttles.

Ripley's Believe It or Not! World's Weirdest Gadgets by Mary Packard. Scholastic, 2002. 3–6. Details include inventors of these strange inventions, quizzes, gadgets made by kids, etc.

Sea Clocks: The Story of Longitude by Louise Borden. Simon & Schuster, 2004. 3–6. For forty years, John Harrison, an Englishman, sought to create the perfect clock to provide sailors with a tool to measure longitude.

So You Want To Be An Inventor? by Judith St. George. Philomel Books, 2002. 3–6. Via their famous inventions, the author describes the characteristics of famous inventors: Charles Goodyear, George Washington, Benjamin Franklin, etc.

Thomas Edison by Jane Shuter. Heinemann Library, 2000. 3–6. Describes the life work of Edison, how to find out more about him, an index and bibliographical references.

Toys! Amazing Stories Behind Some Great Inventions by Don L. Wulffson. Henry Holt & Company, 2000. 3–6. Details the who, what, when, where, how and why of Play Doh®, Silly Putty®, Mr. Potato Head® and many more famous toys.

Where the Sidewalk Ends by Shel Silverstein. HarperCollins, 1973. K–Adult. Humorous poetry collection written from a kid's perspective.

Professional/Reference

Inventing, Inventions, and Inventors: A Teaching Resource Book by Jerry D. Flack. Libraries Unlimited, 1989. Learning options for use with advanced students.

Inventors and Inventions by Lorraine Hopping Egan. Scholastic, 1997. Ideas that incorporate instruction in all curricular areas in grades 4–8. Includes problem-solving, ideas for student inventors, reproducible activity sheets, etc.

Multimedia

Apollo 13. Universal Studios, 2000. VHS/DVD.

Inventions for Students: Computerized Weather Forecasting & Firefighting. Discovery Communications, Inc./Clearvue & SVE, 2004. 3–6. Features the computerized advances that impact weather forecasting and the safety of firefighters on the job.

Inventions for Students: Helpful Inventions. SVE & Churchill Media/Discovery School Channel, 2004. 3–6. Profiles a woman in health care who was inspired to become an inventor by observing how accident victims were treated, and a boy who created an earth-friendly golf tee.

Inventions for Students: The Wright Brothers. SVE & Churchill Media/Discovery School Channel, 2004. 3–6. Biographical account of initial attempts, frustrations and finally the success of the invention of a plane that could actually fly.

Inventors and Inventions. Discovery Channel School, 1997. 3–6. Includes a teacher's guide with a host of activities to do with students from creating a slide show, to viewing video segments for instruction, to interactive participation in computer lab activities, etc.

Web Sites

About.com—Earle Dickson: Inventor of the Band-Aid
inventors.about.com/library/inventors/blbandaid.htm

Camp Invention
www.invent.org/camp_invention/2_1_0_camp.asp
Week-long summer camp program of the National Inventors Hall of Fame appropriate for kids in grades 2–6.

First
www.usfirst.org/jrobtcs/flego.htm
National competition for kids ages 9–14 using Legos to invent things.

Howstuffworks
www.howstuffworks.com
Simple explanations for how all different kinds of things work.

Invention@nationalgeographic.com
www.nationalgeographic.com/features/96/inventions/index.html
Activities include two interactive links: Action Contraption game and It's Your Turn. The latter link offers the opportunity to make your own creation and submit it to National Geographic.

Inventive Kids
www.inventivekids.com/indexFlash.html
Web site chock full of interactive games.

InventorEd, Inc. Presents: Kids Inventor Resources
www.inventored.org/k-12

Lemelson-MIT Program
web.mit.edu/afs/athena.mit.edu/org/i/invent/invent-main.html
The Massachusetts Institute of Technology's Web site that features the Inventor of the Week, the Inventor's Handbook, games, trivia, links and resources.

The Partnership for America's Future, Inc: Specializing in Educational Inventions, Teacher Technique Training, & Competition Development Corporations
www.pafinc.com

United States Patent and Trademark Office: Kids Pages
www.uspto.gov/go/kids
Includes activities sorted by grade level and information: Twinkle Lights K–6; Bright Lights 6–12; and Guiding Lights: Parents, Teachers and Coaches. Some of the links within the Web site offer interactive participation while others provide an excellent insight into the necessity of patents, their history and their impact on society.

Collaboration Notes

_____

_____

_____

_____

_____

_____

_____

_____

_____

_____

_____

_____

_____

_____

_____

_____

_____

_____

_____

_____

Unit 5

Mapping the World: Past, Present & Future

McRel Standards

Economics

- Understands basic concepts about international economics.

Geography

- Understands the characteristics and uses of maps, globes and other geographic tools and technologies.

- Knows the location of places, geographic features and patterns of environment.

- Understands the characteristics and uses of spatial organization of Earth's surface.

- Understands that culture and experience influence people's perceptions of places and regions.

Objectives

- Differentiate between maps, globes and other geographical tools.

- Discuss, review and demonstrate locating a specific place using degrees of latitude and longitude.

- Define the role of a cartographer and a navigator.

- Name the benefits of maps and globes in daily lives.

- Name the seven continents.

Local Objectives

_____

_____

_____

Rationale

Students, as current and/or future travelers in a global society, need to understand that geographic knowledge is essential for planning vacations and future business opportunities.

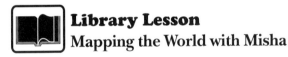 **Library Lesson**
Mapping the World with Misha

Display *Scien-trickery: Riddles in Science.* Introduce it by saying that it has riddles about many things in our everyday world. Challenge students to be ready with their answers after you read the riddle "I'm Lost Without You" on page 21.

Display and introduce the Passport Sack Puppet made from pattern on page 60. Then have the puppet sing its song:

Reading Is Your Passport to the World
(Sung to the theme song of Rawhide.)

Reading, reading, reading,
Keeps you all succeeding,
At home, at school and everywhere.

Don't forget to check books out,
And see what they're about,
Reading is your passport to the world.

Ask the puppet where its travels will take it today. Have the puppet give clues:

1. Continent 10 degrees east by 36 degrees north. Ask the puppet if he means degrees of temperature. When he responds no, that he means navigational degrees for locating a specific place, ask the kids what tool could be used to locate this place. If they don't know, continue with the puppet saying the following clues until the kids guess it correctly or request a map or globe to help them.

2. Continent bordered by the Atlantic and Arctic Oceans.

3. Continent bordered by the Mediterranean, North and Black Seas.

4. Continent west of Asia.

5. Continent east of North America.

6. Continent that includes the countries of England, France, Spain, etc.

Thank Passport for his help and welcome him to stay and share the read-aloud book with the kids.

Display *A Cloak for a Dreamer*. Share that Misha, the main character in the book, loves to travel as much as Passport does. Read the story aloud and point out the clothing and royalty that were, and to some degree still are, a part of European culture. (**Optional:** Play the *World Playground 2* song "Nejha.") Share that if there was a sequel to Misha's book, it might tell of his travels to the continents located at these longitudes and latitudes:

1. 0 degrees longitude by 30 degrees east, _ _ _ _ _ _ (Africa)

2. 45 degrees north by 120 degrees east, _ _ _ _ (Asia)

3. 30 degrees north by 135 degrees east, _ _ _ _ _ _ _ _ _ (Australia)

4. 90 degrees south by 0 degrees, _ _ _ _ _ _ _ _ _ (Antarctica)

5. 45 degrees north by 135 degrees west, _ _ _ _ _ _ _ _ _ _ _ (North America)

6. 15 degrees south by 60 degrees west, _ _ _ _ _ _ _ _ _ _ _ (South America)

Define the role and importance of the job of cartographers. Note that without them all forms of transportation wouldn't have one of the many tools it takes to navigate correctly.

Ask the students if a flat map or a globe is less distorted. Why? Define the meaning of GPS and how, along with many other applications (e.g., OnStar, vehicle theft location capabilities), it has dramatically improved access to navigational process.

Review the lesson by challenging the students to give the names of the imaginary lines (longitude and latitude) that divide the earth for navigational purposes; to name a variety of tools used for navigational purposes (maps, globes, GPS); and to list a variety of ways that these tools impact our daily lives. **Optional:** Close with Passport the puppet singing his reading song.

Bridge Activity 1
Pen Pals Near and Far

Go to www.theteacherscorner.net/penpals and follow the directions listed for locating a grade level and finding a class with which your class can correspond. Please note that requests for finding a class should be done in the fall semester to participate in this Web site's program.

Another option for locating age appropriate pen pals would be to go to the Department of Defense's worldwide school system, www.dodea.edu, then click on Schools, Areas/Districts/Schools, then click for a choice of locations: All Sites, Europe, Pacific, U.S. and Cuba. The screen that appears has every level of schools from elementary through high school so you can pick a level for your students. Have the students generate a variety of questions about the locale the pen pals live in including the longitude and latitude. Use this opportunity to review with students the correct form for letter writing. Since there is a higher cost to send mail to pen pals abroad, you may wish to contact the PTO or a community business to fund the Worldwide Pen Pals Project.

Bridge Activity 2
Navigator's Challenge

Go to www.nationalgeographic.com/geobee and click on Play the Game. Challenge students to take turns answering the questions and to perform the role of navigator using longitude and latitude to locate each place on a wall map, student atlas, globe or other geographical tool.

Bridge Activity 3
Cartographer Extraordinaire

As a whole group activity, go to www.usgs.gov/education and click on Map Wizard, then on Map-It. Follow the instructions to create a Mercator projection map.

A simpler mapmaking lesson, Make-A-Map, for younger students can be accessed by going to teacher.scholastic.com/lessonrepro/lessonplans/profbooks/ss971114b.htm.

Bridge Activity 4
FriendSHIP

Brainstorm a variety of geographical tools that show longitude and latitude: wall maps, globes, student atlases, Web sites, etc. Review the correct way to write degrees of longitude and latitude with students. Discuss the fact that anywhere you go, you can make a friend. Display the pattern from page 61 of the USS FriendSHIP and ask students to complete their ship as follows.

- Top Blank: Write the name of a family, friend or pretend friend who lives on another continent.

- Middle Blank: Write the degrees of longitude and latitude of the location where the person lives.

- Bottom Blank: Leave this blank for a partner to write in the name of the location.

Then pair the students up and have them exchange maps. Their role as navigators is to find the location where that person lives. There are seven different people listed on the hull of each ship. When the students finish, have them exchange papers to check each other's answers. Continue this procedure until all seven sets of blanks have been done. Anytime there is an incorrect answer, ask the partner to circle it and have his or her partner redo the answer.

Classroom Lesson
It Pays to Advertise—Tourist Dollars Needed!

Display a picture of something European or a genuine European item such as money or art. (You could also play music from a European composer such as Mozart.) Explain that many people love to travel and experience living on another continent. Note that countries within the continents often promote tourism to bring in more money for their country.

Have students listen to the highlights covered about the European continent as you read and/or picture talk *Hello, Europe!* and *An Online Visit to Europe.* Record and display the categories of interest for a tourist as detailed in the books. Show the students a travel brochure.

Divide the students into six groups and assign them the job of being the advertising agency hired by the one of the six remaining continents' Bureaus of Tourism to create a brochure the size of a science project display board. The students' objective is to make the continent so inviting that Misha, the main character in *A Cloak for a Dreamer,* would want to visit their continent first. As part of the brochure criteria, remind the students to use only the categories recorded and displayed during the lesson.

Also remind them to include photos and/or illustrations. Give the students the date that the brochures will be displayed and presented to you (you will play the role of Misha).

To assist the students with their research, be sure to provide access to books about continents, not specific countries. If available, provide all of the books from the Internet Field Trips and Our Amazing Continents series from the bibliography, or others like them that do not overwhelm the students with exceptionally detailed information. Instead, the books should focus on the highlights of the continents.

Resources
Books

Fiction

Around the World in 80 Days by Marian Leighton (adaptation of Jules Verne classic). Abdo Publishing, 2002. 5–8.

A Cloak for a Dreamer by Aileen Friedman. Scholastic, 1995. 1–5. Using geometric designs, a tailor father and his apprentice sons are hurriedly making clothing for royalty, but one son's cloak of circles is representative of his dream to travel instead of providing warmth. Mathematical and geographical applications.

Nonfiction

Internet Field Trips series by Erin M. Hovanec. PowerKids Press, 2003. 1–5. Via Internet Web site references, the reader can see the highlights of Africa as if a tourist: climate, geography, natural wonders, animals, countries, people, industry, cultural aspects of art and music plus additional recommended Web sites if you wish to lengthen the journey.

> *An Online Visit to Africa*
> *An Online Visit to Asia*
> *An Online Visit to Australia*
> *An Online Visit to Europe*
> *An Online Visit to North America*
> *An Online Visit to South America*

Maps and Globes (True Books Geography) by David Petersen. Scholastic Library Publishing, 2004. 3–6.

Maps and Journeys by Kate Petty. Barron's, 1993. 3–6. Harry realizes that to create maps and to be able to read them, he needs to use measurement and symbolic drawings.

Maps and Our World by Robert Coupe. Mason Crest Publishers, 2002. 3–6. Pairing simple text with illustrations, children gain an understanding of world populations, geography, resources, climates, countries, climates and plant and animal life from global maps.

Maps: Getting From Here to There by Harvey Weiss. Houghton Mifflin, 1991. 1–4. A comprehensive look at the attributes of maps: the process of making them, latitude and longitude, symbols, charts, distance, directions, etc.

Our Amazing Continents series by April Pulley Sayre. Lerner Publishing Group, 2003. 3–6. A series of seven books, with each volume including superb photographs, limited text and a broad overview of the continent: the people, landforms, weather, plant and animal life.

> *G'day, Australia!*
> *Good Morning, Africa!*
> *Greetings, Asia!*
> *Hello, Europe!*
> *Hooray for Antarctica!*
> *South America, Surprise!*
> *Welcome to North America!*

Scien-trickery: Riddles in Science by J. Patrick Lewis. Silver Whistle, 2004. 1–5. Poetry collection that includes descriptions of various people, places and things in the scientific world.

Small Worlds: Maps and Mapmaking by Karen Romano Young. Scholastic, 2002. 3–6. Comprehensive coverage of types of maps, mapmakers and how the maps are made.

Professional/Reference

Great Map Mysteries: 18 Stories and Maps to Build Geography and Map Skills by Susan Julio. Scholastic Professional Books, 1997.

Multimedia

Globes, Maps & Graphs: Geography Basics. Rainbow Media/United Learning, 2001. VHS. 4–8. Features 3D animation and how maps interpret international topographical features. Also defines and gives examples of latitude and longitude; graphs—bar, line, circle and picture; legends; keys; etc.

Map & Globe Skills. SVE/Churchill Media, 2000. VHS. K–3. Overview and explanation of the basics of creating and utilizing maps, how to read them, how maps differ from globes and the use of geographic grids in everyday life situations.

Map Skills for Children (3 titles in series). Schlessinger Media/Library Video Company, 2004. K–4. Includes footage of Washington, D.C., visiting with cartographers, humor and the evolution of maps to current everyday applications as witnessed by two kids.

World Playground 2. Putamayo World Music, 2001. All grades. CD.

Web sites

BoatSafeKids
www.boatsafe.com/kids/
Click on How'd They Do That—explains how maps and globes are made.

Department of Defense Education Activity
www.dodea.edu
Links will provide listing of campuses for pen pal Bridge activity.

National Geographic.com—GeoBee Challenge
www.nationalgeographic.com/geobee
The GeoBee Challenge offers five new questions each day for kids to answer using geographical locations.

Scholastic—Around the World with Travel Buddies
teacher.scholastic.com/fieldtrp/k2/travel.htm
Stuffed animals travel the world as students track them on the map.

Scholastic—Make-a-Map
teacher.scholastic.com/lessonrepro/lessonplans/profbooks/ss971114b.htm
Lesson plan teaches kids how to create and compare simple maps.

Scholastic—Maps, Globes and Map Skills
teacher.scholastic.com/fieldtrp/socstu/maps.htm
Ideas for teaching map skills as part of a school-year-long teaching tool. Also offers recommended Web sites to extend the learning.

The Teacher's Corner
theteacherscorner.net/penpals
Allows a class to sign up for a grade level appropriate group of pen pals in various places.

USGS Learning Web
www.usgs.gov/education
Click on these links: Maps & Images and Map Wizard (link to Map-It to generate a Mercator projection map by inputting degrees of latitude and longitude).

USGS TerraWeb for Kids: Cool Stuff To Do
terraweb.wr.usgs.gov/TRS/kids/CoolStuffToDo.html
Click on the link to make a pair of 3D glasses and/or Create a 3D Interactive World.

Collaboration Notes

Passport Sack Puppet

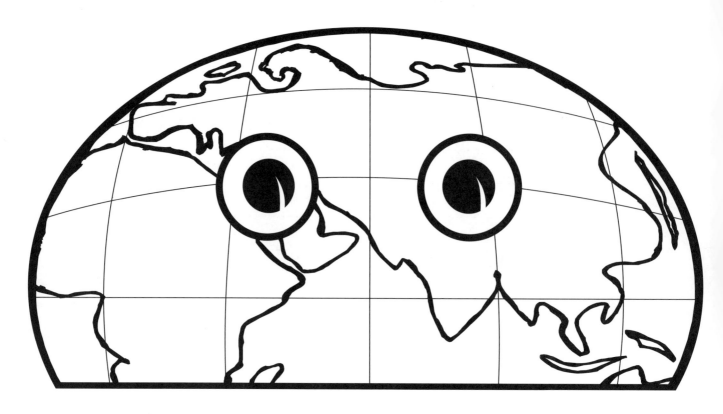

sample puppet

 © 2005 by Aileen Kirkham (UpstartBooks)

Name: _____

Teacher: _____

USS FriendSHIP

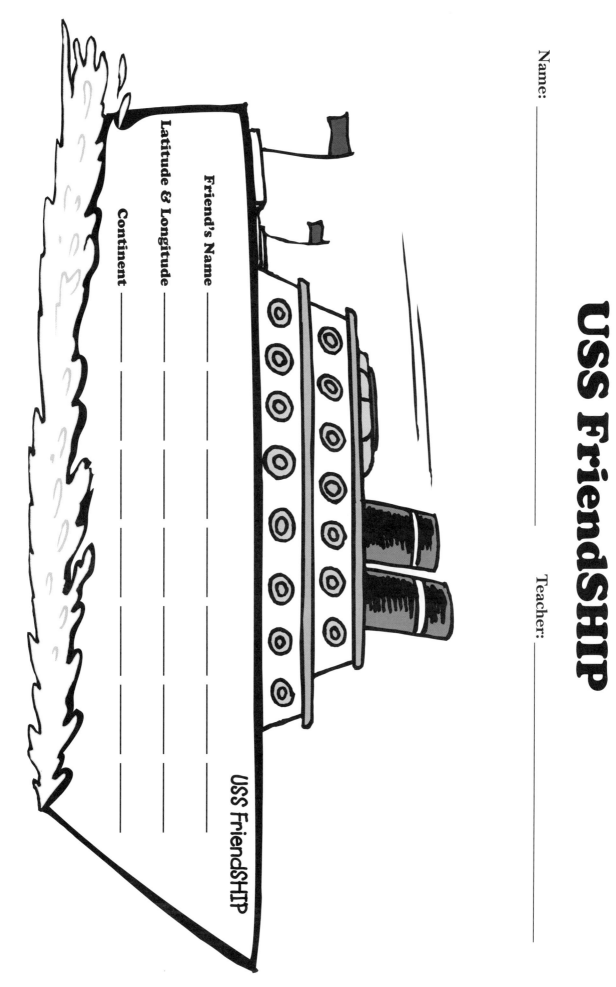

Friend's Name _ _ _ _ _ _ _ _ _ _ _ _

Latitude & Longitude _ _ _ _ _ _ _ _ _ _ _ _

Continent _ _ _ _ _ _ _ _ _ _ _ _

USS FriendSHIP

Tsunamis: Past, Present & Protection

McRel Standards

Geographic

- Knows the location of places, geographic features and patterns of the environment.

- Knows the physical processes that shape patterns on Earth's surface.

- Understands how geography is used to interpret the past.

- Understands global development and environmental issues.

Math

- Understands and applies basic and advanced concepts of statistics and data analysis.

- Understands and applies basic and advanced concepts of probability.

Science

Earth Science

- Understands the Earth's composition and structure.

Physical Science

- Understands the structure and properties of matter.

- Understands the sources and properties of energy.

- Understands forces and motion.

Nature of Science

- Understands the nature of scientific knowledge.

- Understands the nature of scientific inquiry.

Objectives

- Investigate warning systems for tsunamis: human made and animal generated.

- Read dogographies about work dogs that search for victims of natural disasters.

- Use cause and effect logic to understand the dynamics of tsunamis.

- Select research media that is current to date.

- Evaluate Web sites and the validity of their information for research purposes.

- Role-play the job of tsunami scientists who must statistically analyze the possibility of a tsunami hitting their community.

Local Objectives

_____

_____

_____

_____

Rationale

Students, as part of a global society, need the ability to access current and relevant information regarding the locales they plan to visit for pleasure and for a future career in business. As part of their travel research, they should also be apprised of the environmental issues of these locales.

 ## Library Lesson
Internet Dynamics of Tsunami Research

Ask the students to give the appropriate thumb signals so you can assess their understanding of the cause of tsunamis:

- Thumbs up = Tsunamis are weather related.

- Thumbs down = Tsunamis are caused by a force within or outside of planet Earth.

- Thumbs sideways = Don't know.

Instead of telling the students the correct answer, brainstorm a list of various resources, including the Internet, to verify the correct answer. Narrow the list by asking which of the resources would have the most up-to-date information (the Internet, as well as magazines and books with copyrights of 2000–2005). Share with the students that if they choose to use the Internet, they must be sure to validate the information with another source. Display and explain the meanings of Web address abbreviations using Web sites recommended for this unit: www.fema.gov/kids. Note that .gov stands for "government" and is a reliable resource.

Explain that the United States has the Federal Emergency Management Agency, known as FEMA, which was created to inform and help everyone understand the nature of natural disasters and come to their aid as needed. Their money is from the taxpayers and is to be used in the best interest of the taxpayers. Direct the students to view the FEMA Web site, www.fema.gov/kids/. Click on the Disaster Area link and then click on Tsunami. Give the students an opportunity to read the screen, then ask them to answer the same question about a tsunami using thumb signals. To check for comprehension and geographical skills, write this question for everyone to see: Which coast of the United States mainland is at highest risk for tsunamis? If a student answers Hawaii, ask them to rethink their answer by looking for a key word in the question (mainland). (Depending on the age and background of your students, you may need to define the word "mainland".)

Visit the After the Tsunami: How Relief Agencies Work Web site at teacher.scholastic.com/scholasticnews/indepth/tsunami/info/index.asp?article=relief. Note that .com stands for "commercial," meaning a company of private industry. The Web site may or may not be reputable. In other words, .com sites may be less objective than government sites since .com sites are paid for by private businesses and/or their advertisers who want to make as much money as possible.

The Web site at www.nationalgeographic.com/xpeditions/atlas/index.html is a

.com site, but has an excellent reputation in the educational community.

The Web site at www.drgeorgepc. com/TsunamiFAQ.html shares that it is excerpted from UNESCO's World Conference on Natural Disaster Reduction held in Yokohama, Japan, May 23–27, 1994. It should be a reputable source since UNESCO is an organization dedicated to the betterment of the world.

Follow up this introduction to tsunamis by using one of the following resources to give the students a greater understanding of the dynamics of tsunamis.

- View the DVD *Ever-changing Earth for Students: Tsunami*.

- Read aloud *Sweeping Tsunamis*.

- Read aloud *Tsunamis* or *Tsunamis: Killer Waves*.

Go back to the FEMA Web site and click on Photos to show the gigantic buoys that are currently used as an early warning system. Make note that they cost a lot of money and that many of the Asian countries that were hit by the most recent Tsunami on December 26, 2004, had not bought the buoys because they thought the buoys cost too much. Discuss why the countries have changed their minds and why they will make purchasing the buoys a priority.

As a review, have students explain the differences between the Internet addresses found in their research of tsunamis. Ask them to list the four causes of tsunamis: earthquake, slides (land, mud, ice), volcanic eruption and meteorite/asteroid

impact. Query students about what scientists are doing to prevent injury and death from approaching tsunamis. As the students continue to monitor the scientists' future research, ask them how they should evaluate/substantiate what they read about the research on the Internet.

Bridge Activity 1
Danger Detector Puzzle

Go to www.fema.gov/kids and click on Games and Quizzes, then click on Jigsaw Puzzles. Next click on the 96-piece puzzle of the large buoy hanging above the deck. Have individual students or groups of students take turns trying to solve the puzzle. The student who does the puzzle the fastest is proclaimed #1 Danger Detector. Thanks to the #1 Danger Detector the buoy has been built and can now be lowered into the water to detect any seismic disturbances. This will give the community advanced notice should a tsunami head its way.

While students are waiting for a turn to try the puzzle, print out the articles below for the students to read and discuss.

- After the Tsunami: Where Were the Warnings? teacher.scholastic.com/scholasticnews/ indepth/tsunami/warning/index. asp?article = warningsystem

- After the Tsunami: Terrible Quake Hits Southeast Asia teacher.scholastic.com/scholasticnews/ indepth/tsunami/tsunaminews/index. asp?article=quake

- After the Tsunami: Map of the Tsunami Impact
teacher.scholastic.com/scholasticnews/indepth/tsunami/info/index.asp?article=map

Bridge Activity 2
Master of Disaster

Go to www.fema.gov/kids, click on Games & Quizzes, then click on Water, Wind and Earth. Read the directions on how to play with the computer being your opponent. (It's an electronic version of the hand game, Paper, Rock, Scissors, using natural forces.)

Bridge Activity 3
Elephants to the Rescue

Go to teacher.scholastic.com/scholasticnews/indepth/tsunami/warning/index.asp?article=animals. Read what the elephants did in Khao Lak, Thailand, that saved some tourists from the tsunami. Ask the students if they know of any other animal that scientists have used in research (dolphins have heightened sensitivity to certain physical changes in the earth).

Bridge Activity 4
Doggone Great Disaster Hero Cards

Go to www.fema.gov/kids and click on Search. At the search box, type in Canine Heroes. Click on FEMA for Kids: Canine Heroes. Read about the dogs that do an invaluable job of searching for victims of natural disasters like tsunamis. The dogographies are presented in a trading card format.

Classroom Lesson
Tsunami Scientists

Display the American Red Cross symbol and ask the students what it means. Share that disaster preparedness is one of the Red Cross's major goals. Base the lesson on the premise that the class has been contacted to provide statistical data to the Red Cross regarding the probability of a tsunami hitting their community. The class must be able to forecast this chance as a more than 50% possibility or a less than 50% possibility. Tell the students that based upon their findings, the Red Cross will be able to assess the need for a tsunami disaster preparedness program.

As a classroom of tsunami research scientists, facilitate the creation of a time line of tsunamis as listed in the article After the Tsunami: Tsunamis! available at teacher.scholastic.com/scholasticnews/indepth/tsunami/info/index.asp?article=grolier. Remind the students to note on the time line that there may be more than one locale for that date's tsunamis. An example would be the 1960 Chilean earthquake that generated tsunamis traveling to Chile, Hawaii and Japan. The time line should range from 1775 to the most recent on December 26, 2004. (This tsunami is not listed in the article, but can be accessed on the same Web site by changing the last word in the Web site address from "grolier" to "quake.")

Then print the map at www.nationalgeographic.com/xpeditions/atlas/index.UL. Compare it with a globe or wall map, then mark the locales of countries listed on the time line. Discuss that the majority are in the Ring of Fire referenced in the article. Based upon the research in this article, the time line and the map markings, the class must come to a scientific consensus regarding their findings. Have them conduct an open forum to share their findings with the Red Cross liaison (librarian or teacher).

 **Resources**
Books

Nonfiction

Sweeping Tsunamis by Louise Spilsbury. Heinemann Library, 2003. 3–6. Explains the dynamics of a tsunami and details an example: the 1998 tsunami in Papua, New Guinea. It discusses the work of scientists to detect tsunamis for the purpose of creating an international advance warning system. The work of relief agencies who help tsunami victims is also covered.

Tsunamis by Thomas K. Adamson. Capstone Press, 2006. 3–5. Details the dynamics of a tsunami and the consequences of the December 28, 2004, tsunami in the Indian Ocean.

Tsunamis: Killer Waves by Michele Ingber Drohan. PowerKids Press, 2003. 2–5. Explains in very simplistic terminology the dynamics of tsunamis, what people can do to protect themselves and the Pacific warning system.

Professional/Reference

National Geographic. Geographia Special: "Tsunamis—Where Next" and "The World

by Numbers: My Seven." April 2005 issue. Excellent satellite images, photographs, graphs, historical references and text relevant to the dynamics and the impact of the Indian Ocean tsunami on December 28, 2004.

Multimedia

Ever-changing Earth for Students: Tsunami. SVE/Discovery Channel, 2004. VHS/DVD. 1–5. Explains the dynamics and dangers of tsunamis, how to detect them and how scientists research new ways to detect them in the future.

Tsunami: Killer Wave. National Geographic, 2005. DVD. 5–Adult. By revisiting the locales hit by tsunamis, talking with the survivors and referencing the scientific community's research, National Geographic is able to share many details on the dynamics and the catastrophic force of this type of natural disaster.

Web Sites

FEMA for Kids
www.fema.gov/kids
Federal Emergency Management Agency's Web site for kids that covers all kinds of disasters and how to prepare for them. It details the dynamics of each kind of disaster and includes real photos of actual disasters. The Web site also features games, stories, interactive activities, etc.

National Geographic Xpeditions Atlas
www.nationalgeographic.com/xpeditions/atlas/index.html

Scholastic—After the Tsunami: Map of the Tsunami Impact
teacher.scholastic.com/scholastic news/indepth/tsunami/info/index. asp?article=map

Scholastic—After the Tsunami: Terrible Quake Hits Southeast Asia
teacher.scholastic.com/scholasticnews/ indepth/tsunami/tsunaminews/index. asp?article=quake

Scholastic—After the Tsunami: Tsunamis!
teacher.scholastic.com/scholastic-news/indepth/tsunami/info/index. asp?article=grolier

Scholastic—After the Tsunami: Where Were the Warnings?
teacher.scholastic.com/scholasticnews/ indepth/tsunami/warning/index.asp?artic le=warningsystem

The Tsunami Page of Dr. George P. C.
www.drgeorgepc.com/TsunamiFAQ.html
Excerpted from an educational information packet prepared, under contract, for UNESCO for World Conference on Natural Disaster Reduction in Yokohama, Japan, May 23–27, 1994. Title of excerpt is "Tsunami: Frequently Asked Questions About Tsunami and the International Tsunami Warning System."

Collaboration Notes

_____
_____
_____
_____
_____
_____
_____
_____
_____
_____
_____
_____
_____
_____
_____
_____
_____
_____
_____
_____
_____

Bibliography

Fiction Books

Bruchac, Joseph. *Squanto's Journey: The Story of the First Thanksgiving.* Harcourt, 2000.

Bunting, Eve. *How Many Days to America: A Thanksgiving Story.* Houghton Mifflin, 1990.

Cole, Joanna, and Bruce Degen. *The Magic School Bus Inside a Hurricane.* Scholastic, 1995.

Dell, Pamela. *Giles and Metacom: A Story of Plimoth and the Wampanoag.* Tradition Publishing Co., 2002.

Duffey, Betsy. *The Gadget War.* Puffin Books, 1991.

Friedman, Aileen. *A Cloak for a Dreamer.* Scholastic, 1995.

Garland, Sherry. *The Silent Storm.* Harcourt, 1995.

Giff, Patricia Reilly. *Maggie's Door.* Random House, 2003.

Giff, Patricia Reilly. *Nory Ryan's Song.* Bantam Doubleday Dell, 2000.

Gutman, Dan. *The Kid Who Became President.* Scholastic, 1999.

Gutman, Dan. *The Kid Who Ran for President.* Scholastic, 1996.

Hale, Marian. *The Truth About Sparrows.* Henry Holt & Company, 2004.

Hirsch, Beverly. *Annie's Storm.* Cardinal Enterprises of Florida, 1999.

Lake, Julie. *Galveston's Summer of the Storm.* TCU Press, 2003.

Lakin, Pat. *Hurricane!* Lerner Publishing Group, 2000.

Lasky, Kathryn. *Home at Last: Sofia's Immigrant Diary* (Book Two). Scholastic, 2003.

Lasky, Kathryn. *Hope in My Heart: Sofia's Immigrant Diary* (Book One). Scholastic, 2003.

Leighton, Marian. *Around the World in 80 Days* (adaptation of Jules Verne classic). Abdo Publishing, 2002.

London, Jonathan. *Hurricane!* HarperCollins, 1998.

Osborne, Mary Pope. *Thanksgiving on Thursday.* Random House, 2002.

Rogers, Lisa Waller. *The Great Storm: The Hurricane Diary of J. T. King.* Texas Tech University Press, 2002.

Sachar, Louis. *Marvin Redpost: Class President.* Random House, 1999.

Say, Allen. *Grandfather's Journey.* Houghton Mifflin, 1993.

Scieszka, Jon. *Hey Kid, Want to Buy a Bridge?* Viking, 2002.

Taylor, Bonnie Highsmith. *Tragedy from the Sea: the Galveston Hurricane of 1900.* Perfection Learning, 2002.

Wallner, Alexandra. *Sergio and the Hurricane.* Henry Holt & Company, 2000.

Warner, Gertrude Chandler. *Hurricane Mystery.* Albert Whitman & Co., 1996.

Warner, Gertrude Chandler. *The Midnight Mystery.* Albert Whitman & Co., 2003.

Whelan, Gloria. *Goodbye, Vietnam.* Random House, 1993.

Wiesner, David. *Hurricane.* Clarion Books, 1990.

Nonfiction Books

Adamson, Thomas K. *Tsunamis.* Capstone Press, 2006.

Ashby, Ruth. *The Amazing Mr. Franklin or The Boy Who Read Everything.* Peachtree Publishers, 2004.

Barth, Edna. *Turkeys, Pilgrims, and Indian Corn: The Story of the Thanksgiving Symbols.* HarperCollins, 1975.

Berger, Melvin, and Gilda. *Do Tornadoes Really Twist? Questions and Answers About Tornadoes and Hurricanes.* Scholastic, 2000.

Borden, Louise. *Sea Clocks: The Story of Longitude.* Simon & Schuster, 2004.

Bruchac, Joseph. *Pushing Up the Sky: Seven Native American Plays for Children.* Dial, 2000.

Casanellas, Antonio. *Great Discoveries & Inventions that Advanced Industry and Technology.* Gareth Stevens, 2000.

Chambers, Catherine. *Hurricanes.* Heinemann Library, 2000.

Chandra, Deborah, and Madeleine Comora. *George Washington's Teeth.* Farrar, Straus and Giroux, 2003.

Coupe, Robert. *Maps and Our World.* Mason Crest Publishers, 2002.

Davis, Kenneth C. *Don't Know Much About the Pilgrims.* HarperCollins, 2002.

Drohan, Michele Ingber. *Tsunamis: Killer Waves.* PowerKids Press, 2003.

Erlbach, Arlene. *The Kids' Invention Book.* Lerner Publishing Group, 1996.

Freedman, Russell. *Immigrant Kids.* Penguin Putman, 1980.

Freedman, Russell. *Lincoln: A Photobiography.* Clarion Books, 1987.

Gemmell, Kathy. *Storms and Hurricanes.* EDC Publishing, 1996.

Gillis, Jennifer Blizin. *George Eastman.* Heinemann Library, 2004.

Glass, Maya. *Benjamin Franklin: Early American Genius.* Rosen Publishing Group, 2003.

Hall, Margaret. *John Deere.* Heinemann Library, 2004.

Harper, Charise Mericle. *Imaginative Inventions: the Who, What, Where, When, and Why of Roller Skates, Potato Chips, Marbles, and Pie and More!* Little, Brown and Company, 2001.

Hopping, Lorraine Jean. *Wild Weather: Hurricanes!* Scholastic, 1995.

Hovanec, Erin M. Internet Field Trip Series. PowerKids Press, 2003.

> *An Online Visit to Africa*
> *An Online Visit to Antarctica*
> *An Online Visit to Asia*
> *An Online Visit to Australia*
> *An Online Visit to Europe*
> *An Online Visit to North America*
> *An Online Visit to South America*

Ingram, Scott. *The President of the United States.* Blackbirch Press, 2002.

Jones, Charlotte Foltz. *Accidents May Happen.* Bantam Doubleday Dell, 1996.

Jones, Charlotte Foltz. *Mistakes That Worked.* Bantam Doubleday Dell, 1991.

Krull, Kathleen. *Lives of the Presidents: Fame, Shame (and What the Neighbors Thought).* Harcourt, 1998.

Lauber, Patricia. *Hurricanes: Earth's Biggest Storms.* Scholastic, 1996.

Lewis, J. Patrick. *Scien-trickery: Riddles in Science.* Silver Whistle, 2004.

Maestro, Betsy. *Coming to America: The Story of Immigration.* Scholastic, 1996.

McGovern, Ann. *If You Sailed on the Mayflower in 1620.* Scholastic, 1991.

Miller, Raymond H. *Milton Bradley.* Thomson Gale, 2004.

Nobleman, Marc Tyler. *The Light Bulb.* Capstone Press, 2003.

O'Connor, Karen. *Kurdish Family.* Lerner Publishing Group, 1996.

Packard, Mary. *Ripley's Believe It or Not! World's Weirdest Gadgets.* Scholastic, 2002.

Penner, Lucille Recht. *Eating the Plates: A Pilgrim Book of Food and Manners.* Simon & Schuster, 1991.

Petersen, David. *Maps and Globes.* Scholastic Library Publishing, 2004.

Peterson, Tiffany. *Clarence Birdseye.* Heinemann Library, 2003.

Petty, Kate. *Maps and Journeys.* Barron's, 1993.

Provensen, Alice. *The Buck Stops Here: The Presidents of the United States.* HarperCollins, 1990.

Rappaport, Doreen. *We Are the Many: A Picture Book of American Indians.* HarperCollins, 2002.

Reichblum, Charles. *Dr. Knowledge Presents Strange & Fascinating Facts About Famous Brands.* Workman Publishing, 2004.

Samuel, Charlie. *Inventors and Inventions in Colonial America.* PowerKids Press, 2002.

Sanders, Nancy I. *A Kid's Guide to African American History*. Chicago Review Press, 2000.

San Souci, Robert. *N. C. Wyeth's Pilgrims*. Chronicle Books, 1991.

Sayre, April Pulley. Our Amazing Continents Series. Lerner Publishing Group, 2003.
> *G'day, Australia!*
> *Good Morning, Africa!*
> *Greetings, Asia!*
> *Hello, Europe!*
> *Hooray for Antarctica!*
> *South America, Surprise!*
> *Welcome to North America!*

Shuter, Jane. *Thomas Edison*. Heinemann Library, 2000.

Sidman, Joyce. *Eureka! Poems About Inventors*. Lerner Publishing Group, 2002.

Silverstein, Shel. *Where the Sidewalk Ends*. HarperCollins, 1973.

Simon, Seymour. *Hurricanes*. HarperCollins, 2003.

Spilsbury, Louise. *Howling Hurricanes*. Heinemann Library, 2004.

Spilsbury, Louise. *Sweeping Tsunamis*. Heinemann Library, 2003.

St. George, Judith. *So You Want to Be an Inventor?* Philomel Books, 2002.

St. George, Judith. *So You Want to Be President?* Philomel Books, 2000.

Towle, Wendy. *The Real McCoy: The Life of an African-American Inventor*. Scholastic, 1992.

Walsh, Kieran. *Weather Math*. Rourke Publishing LLC, 2004.

Waters, Kate. *Sarah Morton's Day: A Day in the Life of a Pilgrim Girl*. Scholastic, 1991.

Weiss, Harvey. *Maps: Getting From Here to There*. Houghton Mifflin, 1991.

Whitehurst, Susan. *The First Thanksgiving*. PowerKids Press, 2002.

Whitehurst, Susan. *The Mayflower*. PowerKids Press, 2003.

Whitehurst, Susan. *The Pilgrims Before the Mayflower*. PowerKids Press, 2002.

Whitehurst, Susan. *A Plymouth Partnership: Pilgrims and Native Americans*. PowerKids Press, 2002.

Whitehurst, Susan. *Plymouth: Surviving the First Winter*. PowerKids Press, 2002.

Whitehurst, Susan. *William Bradford and Plymouth: A Colony Grows*. PowerKids Press, 2002.

Worland, Gayle. *The Computer*. Capstone Press, 2003.

Wulffson, Don L. *Toys! Amazing Stories Behind Some Great Inventions*. Henry Holt & Company, 2000.

Visconti, Guido. *The Genius of Leonardo*. Barefoot Books, 2000.

Young, Karen Romano. *Small Worlds: Maps and Mapmaking*. Scholastic, 2002.

Professional/Reference Resources

Egan, Lorraine Hopping. *Inventors and Inventions*. Scholastic, 1997.

Flack, Jerry D. *Inventing, Inventions, and Inventors: A Teaching Resource Book*. Libraries Unlimited, 1989.

Julio, Susan. *Great Map Mysteries: 18 Stories and Maps to Build Geography and Map Skills*. Scholastic Professional Books, 1997.

Larson, Erik. *Isaac's Storm: A Man, A Time, and the Deadliest Storm in History*. Vintage Books, 1999.

Library Sparks, November 2003. Vol. 1, No. 3.

> "Thanksgiving Surprise Reader's Theater" by Lois Walker, pages 42–46.

Library Sparks, October 2004. Vol. 2, No. 2.

> "So Many Books ... So Little Time" by Kathleen T. Horning, pages 2–3.

> "Meet the Illustrator: David Small" by TeachingBooks.net, pages 16–21.

> "Paired Readings: Fiction & Nonfiction, Partner with David Small" by Pat Miller, pages 27–31.

> "Vote for Book Clubs" by Laura J. H. Smith, pages 32–35.

"Campaign Slogans," page 47.

"Presidential Nicknames," page 48.

Library Sparks, November 2004. Vol. 2, No. 3.

"Meet Joseph Bruchac" by Rob Reid, pages 6–9.

"Telling Tales, Sharing Lives" by Pat Miller, pages 10–14.

"Native American Heritage Month" by Diane Findlay, pages 30–36.

"Thanksgiving Mad Lib," page 48.

The Mailbox Intermediate: The Idea Magazine for Teachers, Sept. 2004. Vol.26, No.4.

National Geographic. Geographia Special: "Tsunamis—Where Next" and "The World by Numbers: My Seven." April 2005 issue.

Presidents of the U.S. Fact Cards. Toucan Valley Publications, 2001.

Young, Greg. *A Guide for Using the Magic School Bus Inside a Hurricane in the Classroom.* Teacher Created Materials, 1996.

Multimedia

Abraham Lincoln. Nest Entertainment, Inc., 1993. VHS/DVD.

All About Meteorology. Schlessinger Media, 2000. VHS.

Apollo 13. Universal Studios, 2000. VHS/DVD.

Buck, Dennis. *Patriotic Songs & Marches.* Kimbo Educational, 1991. CD.

Ever-changing Earth for Students: Hurricane. Discovery Communications/SVE, Inc., 2004. VHS/DVD.

Ever-changing Earth for Students: Tsunamis. Discovery Communications/SVE, Inc., 2004. VHS/DVD.

Globes, Maps & Graphs: Geography Basics. Rainbow Media/United Learning, 2001. VHS.

Inventions for Students: Computerized Weather Forecasting & Firefighting. Discovery Communications, Inc./ Clearvue & SVE, 2004. VHS/DVD.

Inventions for Students: Helpful Inventions. SVE & Churchill Media/Discovery School Channel, 2004. DVD.

Inventions for Students: The Wright Brothers. SVE & Churchill Media/Discovery School Channel, 2004. DVD.

Inventors and Inventions: The Wright Brothers. SVE & Churchill Media/Discovery School Channel, 2004. VHS/DVD.

Map & Globe Skills. SVE/Churchill Media, 2000. VHS.

Map Skills for Children (3 titles in series). Schlessinger Media/Library Video Company, 2004. VHS/DVD.

Native American Powwow (Come Celebrate With Me Series). SVE & Churchill Media, 2001. VHS.

Songs About America: Celebrating America's History. Kimbo Educational, 2003. CD.

So You Want to Be President? Scholastic/Weston Woods, 2002. VHS.

Stories for Thanksgiving. Scholastic/Weston Woods, 2003. VHS.

Tsunami: Killer Wave. National Geographic, 2005. DVD.

William Bradford: First Thanksgiving (Animated Hero Classics Series). Nest Entertainment, 1992. VHS.

World Playground 2. Putamayo World Music, 2001. CD.

Web sites

About.com—Earle Dickson: Inventor of the Band-Aid
inventors.about.com/library/inventors/blbandaid.htm

An American Thanksgiving
www.night.net/thanksgiving

BoatSafeKids
www.boatsafe.com/kids/

Camp Invention
www.invent.org/camp_invention/2_1_0_camp.asp

Canadian Hurricane Centre Just for Kids!
www.ns.ec.gc.ca/weather/hurricane/kids.html

Department of Defense Education Activity
www.dodea.edu

FEMA for Kids
www.fema.gov/kids

First
www.usfirst.org/jrobtcs/flego.htm

Howstuffworks
www.howstuffworks.com

HyperDictionary
hyperdictionary.com/dictionary/
character+assassination

Invention@nationalgeographic.com
www.nationalgeographic.com/features/96/inventions/index.html

Inventive Kids
www.inventivekids.com/indexFlash.html

InventorEd, Inc. Presents: Kids Inventor Resources
www.inventored.org/k-12

Kid Info
www.kidinfo.com/American_History/
Colonization_Plymouth.html

Lemelson-MIT Program
web.mit.edu/afs/athena.mit.edu/org/i/invent/
invent-main.html

The Mayflower Society
www.mayflower.org

McRel
www.mcrel.org/standards-benchmarks

Merriam-Webster
www.wordcentral.com

Miami Museum of Science & Planetarium
www.miamisci.org/hurricane

National Geographic.com Kids—Flying Into the Eye of a Hurricane
www.nationalgeographic.com/ngkids/0308/hurricane

National Geographic.com Kids—GeoBee Challenge
www.nationalgeographic.com/geobee

National Geographic Xpeditions Atlas
www.nationalgeographic.com/xpeditions/atlas/
index.html

National Oceanic and Atmospheric Administration
hurricanes.noaa.gov/index.html

The Partnership for America's Future, Inc: Specializing in Educational Inventions, Teacher Technique Training, & Competition Development Corporations
www.pafinc.com

Pilgrim Hall Museum
www.pilgrimhall.org/museum.htm

Plimoth Plantation
www.plimoth.org

Scholastic—After the Tsunami: Animals Had Early Warning
teacher.scholastic.com/scholasticnews/indepth/
tsunami/warning/index.asp?article=animals

Scholastic—After the Tsunami: Map of the Tsunami Impact
teacher.scholastic.com/scholasticnews/indepth/
tsunami/info/index.asp?article=map

Scholastic—After the Tsunami: Terrible Quake Hits South Asia
teacher.scholastic.com/scholasticnews/indepth/
tsunami/tsunaminews/index.asp?article=quake

Scholastic—After the Tsunami: Tsunamis!
teacher.scholastic.com/scholasticnews/indepth/
tsunami/info/index.asp?article=grolier

Scholastic—After the Tsunami: Where Were the Warnings?
teacher.scholastic.com/scholasticnews/indepth/
tsunami/warning/index.asp?article=warningsystem

Scholastic—Around the World with Travel Buddies
teacher.scholastic.com/fieldtrp/k2/travel.htm

Scholastic—Hurricanes
teacher.scholastic.com/activities/wwatch/hurricanes/index.htm

Scholastic—Make-a-Map
teacher.scholastic.com/lessonrepro/lessonplans/
profbooks/ss971114b.htm

Scholastic—Maps, Globes and Map Skills
teacher.scholastic.com/fieldtrp/socstu/maps.htm

Suzy Red
www.suzyred.com/quotes.html

The Teacher's Corner
theteacherscorner.net/penpals

The Tsunami Page of Dr. George P. C.
www.drgeorgepc.com/TsunamiFAQ.html

United States Patent and Trademark Office: Kids Pages
www.uspto.gov/go/kids

USGS Learning Web
www.usgs.gov/education

USGS TerraWeb for Kids: Cool Stuff To Do
terraweb.wr.usgs.gov/TRS/kids/CoolStuffToDo.html

Wampanoag History
www.tolatsga.org/wampa.html

Weather Wiz Kids
www.weatherwizkids.com/careercorner.htm

The White House
www.whitehouse.gov/history/presidents/index.html

Yahooligans! Reference: Thesaurus
yahooligans.yahoo.com/reference/thesaurus

Yahooligans! A Web Guide for Kids
yahooligans.yahoo.com/reference/wak/presidents/index.html